THE NATIONAL TRUST

Gardens
Handbook

sponsored by

BURFORD
GARDEN COMPANY

First published in 1991, reprinted 1992
New edition 1993, reprinted 1993
New edition 1995
Completely revised edition published in Great Britain in 2002 by
National Trust (Enterprises) Ltd, 36 Queen Anne's Gate, London SW1H 9AS

ISBN 0 7078 0324 1

www.nationaltrust.org.uk/bookshop

Editor: Liz Dittner
Designed by Pardoe Blacker Ltd, Lingfield, Surrey (2771)

Maps: © Maps in Minutes™ 2001.© Crown Copyright, Ordnance Survey & Ordnance Survey Northern Ireland 2001 Permit No. NI 1675 & © Government of Ireland, Ordnance Survey Ireland.

Printed in China by Wing King Tong Ltd.

Front cover: The circular lily pool, Knightshayes Court
(NTPL/Stephen Robson); detail of one of the herbaceous
borders, The Vyne (NTPL/Andrea Jones)
Back cover: Apple day with the head gardener at Westbury
Court (NTPL/Ian Shaw); a corner of the Jekyll Garden,
Hatchlands (NTPL/Ian Shaw)
Inside back cover (top): The walled kitchen garden,
Beningbrough Hall (NTPL/Stephen Robson)
Title page: Emmetts Garden (NTPL/Leo Mason)
Contents page: Gardener at Sissinghurst Castle
(NTPL/Stephen Robson)

Contents

About the National Trust

The National Trust

- is a registered charity

- is independent of Government

- was founded in 1895 to preserve places of historic interest or natural beauty permanently for the nation to enjoy

- relies on the generosity of its supporters, through membership subscriptions, gifts, legacies and the contribution of many thousands of volunteers

- now protects and opens to the public over 200 historic houses and gardens and 49 industrial monuments and mills

- owns more than 248,000 hectares (612,000 acres) of the most beautiful countryside and almost 600 miles of outstanding coast for people to enjoy

- looks after forests, woods, fens, farmland, downs, moorland, islands, archaeological remains, nature reserves, villages – for ever, for everyone

- has the unique statutory power to declare land inalienable – such land cannot be voluntarily sold, mortgaged or compulsorily purchased against the Trust's wishes without special parliamentary procedure. This special power means that protection by the Trust is for ever

The gardener with visitors at Chartwell (NTPL/Chris King)

- spends all its income on the care and maintenance of the land and buildings in its protection, but cannot meet the cost of all its obligations – four in every five of its historic houses run at a loss – and is always in need of financial support.

Foreword

The National Trust was a late developer as far as gardens were concerned. When the charity was established in 1895 to preserve 'places of natural beauty or historic interest', the properties acquired were small historic buildings such as the Clergy House at Alfriston in Sussex and open spaces such as Brandelhow Park on Derwentwater and Dinas Oleu, a small but significant area of clifftop overlooking Cardigan Bay in Wales. Gardens were not on the agenda at this period.

The first garden to be taken in its own right by the National Trust came in 1946. This was the great garden created by Lawrence Johnston at Hidcote Manor in Gloucestershire. But like a lot of late developers, once the National Trust started to acquire gardens, it warmed to the task, and the result is the wonderful collection that can be seen in the pages of this handbook. Estimates vary as to the number that the Trust now owns, because it is so difficult to define exactly what is meant as a garden, as distinct from parkland or designed landscape. For this book, we have provided details of 147 gardens.

Perhaps the most striking feature of this list is the wide variety, ranging from huge landscaped gardens like Stowe and Stourhead to tiny gems like Mompesson House and Fenton House. Some are very old gardens, such as Westbury Court and Studley Royal, others are historical recreations like Moseley Old Hall. Some are twentieth-century gardens, such as Lady Londonderry's great garden at Mount Stewart, begun in the 1920s, and the famous garden at Sissinghurst Castle, made by Vita Sackville-West and Harold Nicolson in the 1930s.

The first edition of the Gardens Handbook was published in 1991. It is a measure of the popularity of the Trust's gardens that the book has run through several editions. For this new edition,

Polesden Lacey (NTPL/Ian Shaw)

❝ Between them, the National
Trust's gardeners have over
600 years of gardening
experience and expertise. ❞

Chartwell (NTPL/Chris King)

we decided to change the format, and to give the book full colour, so we are grateful to the Burford Garden Company for making this possible by their support. The information contained also reflects the developments that have taken place both in the gardens themselves and in garden visiting.

The National Trust is very aware of the need to be as environmentally friendly as possible. In terms of gardens, this means providing 'green' solutions when practicable. A few Trust

Polesden Lacey (NTPL/Ian Shaw)

gardens, such as Snowshill and Alfriston, are run totally on organic lines, but this is not possible for most properties, cared for by a small number of staff for visitors who expect high standards – including slug-free leaves and blossoms! Over the past few years, however, the National Trust has conducted trials to find alternatives to peat, and now promotes composting and recycling of organic materials within its properties. Many gardens also have areas where organic methods are practised: this book provides information on those properties where, for instance, visitors can buy organic fruit and vegetables.

Visitor figures show that gardens are not only the most popular Trust properties, but also the places most likely to attract repeat visits. All kinds of events are now on offer – meet the gardener, plants sales, walks, and wonderful social occasions like fêtes champêtres and jazz concerts. At some gardens, the visitor season has been extended: at Anglesey Abbey, for instance, there is a Winter Walk and snowdrop weekends take place in February. For each garden featured in this handbook, we have provided information on what can be seen at different times of the year. So go out, visit and enjoy!

How to make the most of your visit

The gardener with visitors at Dudmaston (NTPL/Michael Caldwell)

This handbook has been designed to help you plan and enjoy your visits to some of the most outstanding National Trust gardens.

We have arranged the gardens in alphabetical order. Each entry includes a description of the garden, mentioning its principal features, and giving details of seasonal highlights. We include information on the nature of the garden, soil type, terrain, area and altitude, as well as the number of gardeners employed in its upkeep. Great gardeners associated with the property are mentioned, some of them famous garden designers, others enterprising plantsmen.

How to get there

The maps at the back of this book show the location of the gardens featured in this book, and each garden entry gives a simple grid reference for use with these maps. We also give an Ordnance Survey map reference for each entry and a brief description of the location relative to roads and neighbouring towns.

Over 400,000 plants are propagated annually on Trust properties.

7

Opening times

The opening days and times vary from garden to garden and from year to year. As this is not an annual publication, we have not included details of admission times; the current National Trust Handbook can give you up-to-date information or, as an alternative, the National Trust website, **www.nationaltrust.org.uk** has a searchable directory giving access to property opening times and facilities. The Handbook is distributed free of charge to members but is also sold through bookshops.

Admission prices

National Trust members will normally be admitted free of charge, but please note that even National Trust members may be asked to pay an entry fee on special National Gardens Scheme (NGS) days (see page 10). Admission prices, as well as opening dates and times, can be found in the current National Trust Handbook. The information can also be found on the National Trust website at **www.nationaltrust.org.uk**

Spring plant fair at Petworth
(NTPL/David Levenson)

Anglesey Abbey in Cambridgeshire boasts the largest collection of National Trust garden statuary – a startling 104 statues.

Westbury Court Garden in Gloucestershire, has a Holm Oak planted *circa* 1600, thought to be the oldest in the UK.

Spring plant fair at Petworth (NTPL/David Levenson)

Facilities

Symbols indicate the presence at the property of facilities such as parking, refreshments, shop and WCs. The Trust is constantly working to improve the facilities offered to visitors, so for up-to-date information please consult the current National Trust Handbook, or our main website, **www.nationaltrust.org.uk**

Visitors with disabilities

For users of wheelchairs we give a brief assessment of accessibility based on the type of terrain, degree of slope, width of pathways, etc. We have tried to indicate the availability of adapted WCs but properties are constantly working to improve the quality of facilities offered, and it is therefore advisable to check with the relevant property before your visit. Many of the gardens offer areas with scented plants, and Braille guides are increasingly available.

Although dogs are seldom admitted to National Trust gardens or parks, dogs assisting visitors with disabilities are normally welcome as long as they are in harness during the visit. A free booklet, giving general information for visitors with disabilities, is available from the National Trust Membership Department, FREEPOST MB 1438, Bromley, Kent BR1 3BR. Please enclose a first-class stamp and an addressed label.

Special features

For visitors with special interest in particular garden features, such as water gardens, orangeries and conservatories, rock gardens, roses or fruit and vegetables, we have listed these at the back of the book in an easy-to-use format. We have also given details of National Council for the Conservation of Plants and Gardens (NCCPG) National Collections in National Trust gardens.

> There are almost 100,000 trees on National Trust properties, with 9,575 planted each year.

Plant sales

Plants are on sale at many of the gardens, and where possible we have included this information in the entry. Some gardens have a dedicated plant centre; others sell plants only at open days, plant fairs or other seasonal events.

Events

Many National Trust gardens hold special events, ranging from plant fairs and apple days to open-air concerts and theatre, and we give an indication of these in the entries. Further details of events can be found on the National Trust website at **www.nationaltrust.org.uk** in the Things to do section.

National Gardens Scheme (NGS) Days

Each year, many of the National Trust's gardens are opened on extra days in support of the National Gardens Scheme. Members of the National Trust may have to pay for entry on NGS days. Money raised is donated to support nurses' and gardeners' charities, including National Trust gardens, where it is used primarily for the provision of garden apprenticeships. The National Trust acknowledges with gratitude the generous and continuing support of the National Gardens Scheme Charitable Trust.

The National Trust Gardeners' Apprenticeship Scheme

The conservation and restoration of historic gardens would be impossible without gardeners trained in the professional skills required to understand and maintain the character of each individual garden. To ensure that this knowledge is not lost but handed down from one generation to the next, the National Trust runs its own three-year gardeners' apprenticeship scheme, Careership, providing practical training under the supervision of experienced Trust staff, together with college tuition.

Each year, the Trust recruits twelve salaried apprentices, five of whom are funded through bursaries from the National Gardens Scheme. Careership is open to anyone over the age of sixteen, and draws students from a variety of backgrounds and ages, including many who are seeking a career change. Many students continue their careers as National Trust gardeners, eventually becoming Head Gardeners, while other graduates have gone on to work at horticultural organisations such as the Botanic Gardens of Edinburgh and Bristol, Rosemoor (RHS) and the John Innes Centre.

For further information about Careership contact the National Trust on 0870 458 4000.

The National Trust Online

If you have not yet discovered the National Trust's website then do take a look! It can be found at **www.nationaltrust.org.uk** and is full of information designed to keep you up to date with the Trust. A searchable directory gives you access to property opening times and facilities, and you can read about current news and forthcoming events. There is also educational information and an online bookshop through which you can order a comprehensive range of National Trust books, plus links to other organisations and much more. We are continuing to develop our website, so do check back from time to time to see what is happening. In addition, this handbook contains details of those properties which can be contacted direct by email – see individual entries for more information. General email enquiries should be sent to **enquiries@thenationaltrust.org.uk**

Volunteers

The care and presentation of Trust gardens require considerable effort by the gardening teams, more than a 1,000 of whom are volunteers. Many are gardening enthusiasts who work along-side gardeners, or they may be young people gaining practical experience for a future career in horticulture. The majority of garden volunteers act as stewards, welcoming thousands of visitors every year, giving guided walks and pointing out features of special interest. Information on volunteer opportunities in the gardens, houses and offices of the National Trust can be found on our website: **www.nationaltrust.org.uk/volunteers**

Working holidays

The Trust hosts some 400 Working Holidays on coast and countryside properties throughout England, Wales and Northern Ireland, but you can also join National Trust gardeners at a number of properties. For the experienced or novice gardener this is an opportunity to learn from the experts and see a different side of National Trust gardens. There is a wide variety of holidays for ages 17 to 70. For a brochure call 0870 429 2428.

Gardener working on carpet bedding at Cragside
(NTPL/Joe Cornish)

Acorn Bank Garden

Charming walled garden protected by fine oaks, under which grows a vast display of daffodils. A new orchard was planted 1999-2000 with local apple varieties; produce is used in the tea-room and is sold on Apple Days.

Surrounding the orchards are mixed borders with herbaceous plants, shrubs and roses. The herb garden has the most comprehensive collection of culinary and medicinal plants in the north of England. The sunken garden, with pond and dry-stone terrace, is being restored using 1940s photographs. Woodlands walks have been re-established through the wildlife garden, with the introduction of a wildlife pond. Greenhouse.

Apr	daffodils
May	blossom, newts (sunken garden pond)
Jun	herb garden, newts
Jul	mixed borders
Aug	mixed borders
Sep	late clematis
Oct	apples
Win	closed

Temple Sowerby, nr Penrith, Cumbria CA10 1SP
Tel 017683 61893
Fax 017683 61467
Email acornbank@ntrust.org.uk

Location (7:E5) Just N of Temple Sowerby, 6ml E of Penrith on A66 [91: NY612281]

Soil Clay loam

Terrain Gently sloping site for walled garden, steep slope in wild garden

Altitude 75m/246ft

Area 1 hectare/2 acres

Gardeners 1 full-time

Great gardeners Graham Stuart Thomas

[&] Partially accessible

[@] Braille guide, scented plants, guide dogs allowed

[K] Woodland walk only

Events Apple Days – produce for sale on Apple Days only

Other gardens in the area
Wordsworth House
Dalemain (not NT)
Hutton-in-the-Forest (not NT)
Larch Cottage Nurseries (not NT)

One of the mixed flower borders
(NTPL/Clive Boursnell)

13

Alfriston Clergy House

Apr	spring bulbs
May	Judas tree
Jun	old roses, scented pinks
Jul	old roses
Aug	herbaceous
Sep	sunflowers, hollyhocks
Oct	fruit
Win	closed Dec–Feb

The Tye, Alfriston, Polegate,
Sussex BN26 5TL
Tel 01323 870001
Fax 01323 871318
Email alfriston@ntrust.org.uk

Location (2:H8) 4ml NE of Seaford, just E of B2108, in Alfriston village, adjoining The Tye and St Andrew's Church [189: TQ521029]

A picture-postcard, 14th-century thatched house and small garden set in tranquil Cuckmere Valley. The garden is divided into small 'rooms' with cottage borders and old-fashioned roses, a sunken herb garden, 'potager' vegetable garden and orchard. Fine views along the river valley from the brick terraces and a good deal of wildlife interest. Largely organic. The garden continues to mature within the framework laid out in the 1920s by Sir Robert Witt, who was tenant at the time. Magnificent Judas tree.

Soil Alkaline, light soil

Terrain South facing & level terrace, susceptible to flooding

Altitude 5.5m/18ft

Area 0.5 hectares/1 acre

Gardeners 1 part-time

   Partially accessible

   Braille guide, scented plants, guide dogs allowed

Events Evening garden tours

Other gardens in the area
Bateman's
Sheffield Park Garden
Michelham Priory (not NT)

The 'potager' vegetable garden (NTPL/Andrew Butler)

14

Anglesey Abbey

The garden was developed from 1926 by the 1st Lord Fairhaven, presenting an imposing blend of formal 17th-century French-style and 18th-century natural landscaping. Majestic tree-lined avenues and walks form the framework for hidden, more formal gardens such as the dahlia garden and a semi-circular herbaceous garden. Lord Fairhaven's impressive collection of statuary is positioned throughout the grounds and features in the garden layout. Many rare and unusual tree species on arboretum lawns and the parkland. More recently a large collection of snowdrops (*Galanthus*) has been established throughout the gardens along with an area on the eastern side dedicated to plants giving winter interest. The Winter Garden's serpentine path links into a mile-long circuit through the grounds.

Apr	hyacinths, spring bulbs
May	cowslips, blossom
Jun	herbaceous border, wild flowers
Jul	herbaceous border, wild flowers, dahlias
Aug	dahlias, herbaceous border, specimen trees
Sep	dahlias, autumn colour
Oct	autumn colour, winter garden
Win	snowdrops, early spring bulbs

Lode, Cambridge,
Cambridgeshire CB5 9EJ
Tel/Fax 01223 811200 (property information) · 01223 811243 (office)
Email
angleseyabbey@ntrust.org.uk

Location (4:F6) 6ml NE of
Cambridge on B1102
[154: TL533622]

Galanthus ' Ailwyn', from the Anglesey snowdrop collection
(NTPL/Stephen Robson)

Soil Alkaline sandy loam

Terrain Level

Altitude 30m/98ft

Area 42 hectares/104 acres

Gardeners 6 full-time

Fully accessible

 Scented plants, guide dogs allowed, (braille guide in house only)

Plant sales All year

Events All year. Tel. for a leaflet

Other gardens in the area
Wimpole Hall
University Botanic Garden,
  Cambridge (not NT)

Antony

Apr	rhododendrons, azaleas, camellias, magnolias
May	rhododendrons, azaleas, camellias, wild flowers
Jun	summer garden, day-lilies
Jul	summer garden, day-lilies, roses
Aug	summer garden, roses, magnolias
Sep	summer garden, roses
Oct	autumn colour
Win	closed

Torpoint, Plymouth, Cornwall
PL11 2QA
Tel/Fax 01752 812364
Email antony@ntrust.org.uk

Location (1:E8) 5ml W of
Plymouth via Torpoint car ferry,
2ml NW of Torpoint, N of A374,
16ml SE of Liskeard, 15ml E of
Looe [201: SX418564]

Soil Lime free

Terrain Slope to River Lynher

Altitude 30m/98ft

Area 40 hectares/99 acres

Gardeners 3 full-time

Great gardeners Humphry
Repton

 Partially accessible

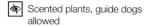 Scented plants, guide dogs
allowed

Events Lions Fair, Church Fair,
Day-Lily Day

Other gardens in the area
Cotehele
Saltram
Mount Edgcumbe (not NT)

Antony's formal gardens, set in a Repton landscape
with beautiful views to the River Lynher, feature
lawns, hedges, a summer garden, small Japanese garden,
terraces, a knot garden and borders with roses and
mixed shrubs. There are many fine trees, including a
magnificent black walnut and 'champion trees' *Ginkgo
biloba* and cork oak. There is also an extensive National
Collection of day-lily with 610 cultivars. The Woodland
Garden (not NT but admission free to NT members
on days when the house is open) contains the National
Collection of *Camellia japonica* (300 cultivars), beautiful
magnolias, rhododendrons, fine trees and shrubs, wild
flowers and river walks. Sculptures can be found in
both the formal and woodland parts of the garden.

'Hypercone' by Simon Thomas, in the summer garden
(NTPL/Derek Croucher)

Apprentice House Garden, Quarry Bank Mill

A working kitchen garden set in the time of the industrial revolution. It illustrates how life would have been for the pauper children who came to work in the cotton mill and also had to grow their own food. Nowadays the produce, which is organically grown, is supplied to the Mill Restaurant. Vegetables are grown all year round using seed from before 1900 and from endangered varieties. The garden has strong links with the Heritage Seed Library (HDRA). The orchard contains many local varieties of fruit and there is a large collection of herbs for medicinal and domestic use. The traditional methods used in the garden include many country crafts, while hens and geese roam the orchard. All combine to create a busy, friendly place to visit for anyone interested in gardening and history.

Leeks in the kitchen garden (NTPL/Mike Williams)

Apr	seasonal vegetables, herbs
May	seasonal vegetables, herbs
Jun	seasonal vegetables, herbs
Jul	fruit crops
Aug	fruit crops
Sep	seasonal vegetables, herbs
Oct	seasonal vegetables, herbs
Win	seasonal vegetables, herbs

Wilmslow, Cheshire SK9 4LA
Tel 01625 527468
Fax 01625 539267
Email
quarrybankmill@ntrust.org.uk

Location (7:L7) 1½ml N of Wilmslow off B5166, 2½ml from M56, exit 5, 10ml S of Manchester [109: SJ835835]

Soil Sandy loam/clay loam

Terrain Slight rises, mostly flat

Altitude 96m/315ft

Area 0.6 hectares/1 acre

Gardeners 2 part-time

Partially accessible

Guide dogs allowed

Events Herb Week, Apple Day and Pruning Day

Other gardens in the area
Dunham Massey
Lyme Park
Tatton Park

Ardress

Apr	spring flowers
May	apple blossom
Jun	roses
Jul	roses
Aug	herbaceous borders
Sep	herbaceous borders
Oct	orchard
Win	closed

64 Ardress Road, Portadown,
Armagh BT62 1SQ
Tel/Fax 028 3885 1236
Email ardress@ntrust.org.uk

Location (1:G6) [H914559]

Soil Lough Neagh basin clay

Terrain Flat

Altitude 100-130m/328-427ft

Area 1.5 hectares/4 acres

Gardeners 1 part-time

⬛ Partially accessible

⬛ Guide dogs allowed

⬛ dogs allowed on leads

Events Spring annual Apple
Blossom Day, Ghostly
Hallowe'en and Apple Fair in
October

Other gardens in the area
The Argory
Parkanaur Forest Park (not NT)
Peatlands Park (not NT)

An attractive small garden with woodland and riverside walks. Terraced flower garden with small formal rose garden planted with early Irish roses and with a 1790 oval Coade urn as a centrepiece, decorated with grapes and leopards' heads. There is a working orchard, with specimens of old Irish varieties of apple trees. These are a speciality as the garden has the NCCPG National Collection of traditional Irish apples, and events include an annual Apple Blossom Day in spring and an Apple Fair in October. There are no longer any animals at Ardress, but there is a display of traditional farming tools and dairy equipment centred around a very pretty courtyard. From the children's playground there are splendid views over the orchards of Co. Armagh.

The garden in front of the house (NT/Roger Kinkead)

The Argory

A beautiful setting overlooking the River Blackwater, with 19th-century pleasure grounds including ancient oak-woods, a lime walk and riverside walks, two yew arbours and a large Tulip tree. Wrought-iron gates lead into a small rose garden planted with old varieties enclosed by privet hedging in separate beds with a sundial in the centre. These beds have been replanted by the Trust using small-flowered China and polyantha roses. Three borders contain specimen shrubs and there is a large ha-ha retaining wall with two summer-houses.

Apr	rhododendrons
May	rhododendrons
Jun	tulip tree, wistaria
Jul	roses
Aug	pleasure grounds
Sep	autumn colour
Oct	autumn colour
Win	snowdrops

Moy, Dungannon, Armagh
BT71 6NA
Tel 028 8778 4753
Fax 028 8778 9598
Email argory@ntrust.org.uk

Location (1:G6) 4ml from Moy, 3ml from M1, exit 13 or 14 (signposted). NB coaches must use exit 13; weight restrictions at Bond's Bridge [H872580]

Soil Lough Neagh basin clay

Terrain Low-lying, flat

Altitude 25m/82ft

Area 2 hectares/5 acres

Gardeners 1 full-time

Partially accessible

Scented plants, guide dogs allowed

dogs allowed on leads

Plant sales Spring plant fair

Events Regular guided woodland walks

Other gardens in the area
Ardress
Parkanaur Forest Park (not NT)
Peatlands Park (not NT)

Old varieties of roses in the sundial garden
(NTPL/Christopher Gallagher)

Arlington Court

Apr	spring bulbs
May	rhododendrons
Jun	azaleas
Jul	herbaceous borders
Aug	herbaceous borders, bedding
Sep	Victorian garden, walled garden
Oct	autumn colour
Win	woodland walks, camellias, winter bedding

Arlington, nr Barnstaple, Devon
EX31 4LP
Tel 01271 850296
Fax 01271 850711
Email arlingtoncourt@ntrust.org.uk

Location (1:F5) 8 ml NE of
Barnstaple on A39
[180: SS611405]

Garden of early 19th-century house in parkland setting with lawns, wilderness pond, spring bulbs and wild flowers. Formal Victorian garden consisting of herbaceous beds and annual borders with raised circular beds and a conservatory.

The partially restored walled kitchen garden is mostly laid down to grass at present, and the perimeter border produces a broad selection of vegetables. Apples, pears, plums and nectarines are trained against the walls. Fruit cage, rebuilt lean-to greenhouse. Also collection of recently planted species of *Fraxinus* (ash). The garden and house were given to the NT in 1949 by Miss Rosalie Chichester.

Soil Light acid soil, overlaying slate

Terrain Mostly flat, exposed to wind

Altitude 243m/797ft

Area 12 hectares/30 acres

Gardeners 2 full-time

 Partially accessible

 Braille guide, scented plants, guide dogs allowed

dogs allowed on leads

Events Folk Festival (August), NGS garden guided walks May/July, Hallowe'en walk

Other gardens in the area
Dunster Castle
Killerton House
Knightshayes
Marwood Gardens (not NT)
Rosemoor RHS garden (not NT)

The formal Victorian garden
(NTPL/Derek Croucher)

Ascott

The garden at Ascott has always been one of its best-known and most original features. Surrounding a Rothschild house, it combines Victorian formality with 20th-century natural style. Terraced lawns, offering panoramic views across the Chilterns, are dotted with specimen and ornamental trees. The impressive topiary includes a giant evergreen sundial planted in gold and dark Irish yew. The Dutch Garden, a long, narrow enclosure surrounded by shrubby banks and clipped hedges, contains formal beds for spring and summer schemes, with a fountain carrying a statue of Eros by the American sculptor Thomas Waldo Story. The Madeira Walk, a long border divided into formal and informal planting, shelters frost-tender shrubs and climbers. Fountains include Story's extravagant bronze Venus. Lily pond.

Apr	spring bulbs, daffodils
May	magnolias
Jun	summer bedding
Jul	herbaceous border
Aug	herbaceous border
Sep	autumn foliage
Oct	closed
Win	closed

Wing, nr Leighton Buzzard,
Buckinghamshire LU7 0PS
Tel 01296 688242
Fax 01296 681904
Email info@ascottestate.co.uk

Location (2:E3) ½ml E of Wing,
2ml SW of Leighton Buzzard, on
S side of A418 [165: SP891230]

Soil Clay

Terrain Terraced

Altitude 125m/410ft

Area 12 hectares/30 acres

Gardeners 6 full-time, 2 part-time, 2 seasonal

Great gardeners Harry Veitch

 Partially accessible

Scented plants, guide dogs allowed

Other gardens in the area
Claydon House
Waddesdon Manor
Woburn Abbey (not NT)

Venus in her shell chariot in the circular garden
(NTPL/Vera Collingwood)

Attingham Park

Apr	daffodils
May	rhododendrons, azaleas
Jun	
Jul	
Aug	
Sep	
Oct	autumn colour
Win	snowdrops

Shrewsbury, Shropshire SY4 4TP
Tel 01743 708162
Fax 01743 708175
Email attingham@ntrust.org.uk

Location (6:B6) 4ml SE of
Shrewsbury, on N side of B4380
in Atcham village
[126: SJ550099]

A plate from Humphry Repton's
'Red Book', showing his
proposed improvements to the
18th-century landscape
(NTPL/John Hammond)

An 18th-century landscape designed by Humphry Repton to complement the vast mansion at Attingham. The NT's management of the property follows closely Repton's 'Red Book' for Attingham. The pleasant Mile Walk takes the visitor along the River Tern past a variety of trees and shrubs. More recent plantings have taken into account historical lists of shrubs prepared in 1770 by Thomas Leggett. The path continues past the orchard, gardeners' cottages (now housing a landscape exhibition) and walled garden. Another walk leads through the deer park and Attingham Woods.

Soil Mixed light soil

Terrain Flat, sheltered

Altitude 30m/98ft

Area 20 hectares/49 acres

Gardeners 2 full-time

Great gardeners Humphry Repton

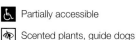 Partially accessible

Scented plants, guide dogs allowed

dogs allowed on leads, but not in deer park

Plant sales May

Events Various guided walks

Other gardens in the area
Benthall Hall
Berrington Hall
Dudmaston
Erddig
Powis Castle
Sunnycroft

Avebury Manor

Parts of the manor may date back to the Benedictine priory, known to have existed in the 12th century. The garden was completely redesigned in the early 20th century by Colonel and Mrs Jenner. Medieval walls surround a series of enclosed 'rooms' containing raised walks, flower gardens, an orchard with bulbs and a rose garden. Some of the walls and hedges are very old and may be survivals of the original priory precinct. Fish-ponds originally occupied an adjoining meadow.

Apr	bulbs
May	spring flowering shrubs
Jun	roses
Jul	herbaceous, bedding, topiary
Aug	herbaceous, bedding, topiary
Sep	herbaceous, bedding, topiary
Oct	herbaceous, bedding, topiary
Win	closed

Soil Poor shallow soil over chalk

Terrain Level

Altitude 158m/518ft

Area 2.4 hectares/6 acres

Gardeners 2 full-time

Great gardeners Vita Sackville-West

  Fully accessible

  Guide dogs allowed

Other gardens in the area
The Courts
Dyrham Park
Lacock Abbey
Bowood House (not NT)

nr Marlborough, Wiltshire
SN8 1RF
Tel 01672 539250
Fax 01672 539388
Email avebury@ntrust.org.uk

Location (1:L4) 6ml W of Marlborough, 1ml N of the Bath road (A4) on A4361 and B4003 [SU099700]

An armillary sphere in the garden in front of the manor (NTPL/David Noton)

23

Baddesley Clinton

Apr	bulbs, wild flowers
May	wallflowers, wistaria, clematis, peonies
Jun	mixed border, herbs, irises
Jul	mixed border, herbs, roses
Aug	dahlias, mixed border, herbs, sweet peas
Sep	dahlias, pampas grasses, water lilies
Oct	dahlias, crinum
Win	bulbs, wild flowers

Rising Lane, Baddesley Clinton
Village, Knowle, Solihull,
Warwickshire B93 0DQ
Tel 01564 783294
Fax 01564 782706
Email
baddesleyclinton@ntrust.org.uk

Location (6:E8) ¾ml W of A4141
Warwick–Birmingham road, at
Chadwick End, 7½ml NW of
Warwick, 6ml S of M42 junction
5; 15ml SE of central
Birmingham [139: SP199715]

Soil Clay/Mercia mudstone grit
subsoil pH7

Terrain Level formal courtyard
gardens, walled garden, meadow
sloping to Great Pool

Altitude 115m/377ft

Area 4.5 hectares/11 acres

Gardeners 2 full-time

[symbol] Fully accessible

[symbol] Scented plants, guide dogs
allowed

Plant sales Plant sales table,
and a stall at Packwood House
Spring Plant Fair

Timeless garden of ancient moated manor, with walled garden, formal courtyard garden, wildflower meadow, woodland/lakeside walks, stew ponds and Long Ditch (medieval). The walled garden, dating from the early 18th century, contains a restored sundial with surrounding borders of shrub roses. All-year interest in the planting schemes, with emphasis on herbs, annuals, climbers (wistaria, clematis), dahlias and a mixed border. A new thatched summer-house opened in 2001 in the corner of the walled garden, fronted by two herb borders. One of the lean-to Victorian greenhouses has been restored. The Japanese-style ornamental bridge over the Long Ditch opened in 2000, linking the stewponds and nature trail areas. A loving seat, in Forest of Dean stone, depicts local wildlife.

Other gardens in the area
Packwood House
Upton House Gardens
Elizabethan Knot Garden,
 Knowle Library (not NT)

Lord Leycester Hospital Gardens
 (not NT)
Ryton Gardens (HDRA) (not NT)
Warwick Castle Gardens (not NT)

Sweet peas in the mixed border
(NTPL/Andrew Butler)

Barrington Court

Barrington Court garden was laid out in the 1920s for the Lyle family to designs by architects J. E. Forbes, who used basket-weave brick paths and fine masonry in walls and outhouses to give the garden structure. Gertrude Jekyll advised on the planting of this varied and enchanting garden laid out in a series of contrasting 'rooms'. A lovely white garden has been added by the present head gardener, Christine Brain. Seasonal fruit and vegetables are tended in the walled kitchen garden and used in the restaurant.

Apr	daffodils, magnolias, wallflowers
May	lily garden, azaleas, roses
Jun	kitchen garden, kniphofia, clematis
Jul	herbaceous, phlox, roses
Aug	white garden
Sep	lily garden, asters, dahlias
Oct	conkers, orchards
Win	daffodils

Soil Silty clay loam pH6.5

Terrain Level

Altitude 20m/66ft

Area 19 hectares/47 acres

Gardeners 3 + 1 careership full-time

Great gardeners Gertrude Jekyll

 Fully accessible

Scented plants, guide dogs allowed

Plant sales All season

Other gardens in the area
Lytes CaryManor
Montacute
Tintinhull
Avon Bulbs (not NT)
East Lambrook (Margery Fish) (not NT)
Hatch Court (not NT)
Hestercombe (not NT)
Lower Severalls (not NT)

Barrington, nr Ilminster, Somerset TA19 0NQ
Tel 01460 241938
Fax 01460 242614
Email barringtoncourt@ntrust.org.uk

Location (1:J6) In Barrington village, 5ml NE of Ilminster, on B3168. M5 (Junction 25) A358 4ml, then follow signs. If approaching from either direction on A303 leave at Hayes End roundabout from where property is signposted [193:ST396182]

Below: One of Barrington's characteristic brick paths leading into the next 'room'

Above: Terracotta forcing pots in the kitchen garden (NTPL/Neil Campbell-Sharp)

Bateman's

Apr	spring borders, wild flowers
May	spring borders, wild flowers
Jun	roses, mulberry garden
Jul	roses, mulberry garden
Aug	roses, mulberry garden
Sep	
Oct	
Win	wild garden March w/ends

Burwash, Etchingham, Sussex
TN19 7DS
Tel 01435 882302
Fax 01435 882811
Email batemans@ntrust.org.uk

Location (2:H7) ½ml S of
Burwash (A265); approached by
road leading S from W end of
village or N from Woods Corner
(B2096) [199: TQ671238]

Rudyard Kipling lived at Bateman's from 1902 until his death in 1936, and the Kiplings did much to create the peaceful garden that now surrounds the Jacobean house, planting hedges, laying paths and planning the rose garden. A pear alley planted with old pears interspersed with clematis, is trained to form a tunnel with shade-tolerant plants underneath. The mulberry garden has box-edged borders of shrubs and perennials, and spring borders designed by Graham Stuart Thomas. The walk to the mill house by the river is edged with cherries, amelanchier, wild flowers and spring bulbs. Pond designed for young children to use for swimming and boating.

Soil Lime-free

Terrain South facing, sloping and level

Altitude 75m/246ft

Area 4 hectares/10 acres

Gardeners 2 full-time

Great gardeners Graham Stuart Thomas

Fully accessible

Scented plants, guide dogs allowed

Other gardens in the area
Scotney Castle
Sissinghurst Castle

The pond and lime avenue, looking towards the house
(NTPL/Stephen Robson)

Belton House

When Sir John Brownlow built the house in the 1680s, he may well have commissioned Captain William Winde, a military man turned architect, to lay out the formal gardens. A devastating flood and and the new fashion for 'natural' landscape combined to sweep away this scheme, leaving only a small canal to the north-east of the house. But later generations of Brownlows were to return to the original formal idea: the sunken Italian garden, designed by Jeffry Wyatville at the beginning of the 19th century; and the Dutch garden commissioned by the 3rd Earl Brownlow in 1880 to harmonise with the north front of the house.

Recently the gardens have benefited from extensive work – Wyatville's orangery restored, walls and garden features repaired, shrubberies replanted, and the recreation of the statue walk and box maze.

Apr	spring flowers, spring bedding
May	bluebells, spring bedding
Jun	flowering plants in Orangery
Jul	herbaceous borders, summer bedding
Aug	herbaceous borders, summer bedding
Sep	summer bedding
Oct	autumn foliage
Win	closed, but open for Snowdrop Sunday; spring bulbs and wild flowers

Detail of the Italian garden (NTPL/Nick Meers)

Grantham, Lincolnshire
NG32 2LS
Tel 01476 566116/592900
Fax 01476 579071
Email belton@ntrust.org.uk

Location (5:D6) 3ml NE of Grantham on A607 Grantham–Lincoln road, easily reached, and signposted from A1 [130: SK929395]

Soil Light, sandy

Terrain Flat terrain, exposed site with partial frost pocket. Surrounded by undulating land.

Altitude 50m/164ft

Area 13.3 hectares/33 acres

Gardeners 4 full-time

Great gardeners William Emes, Jeffry Wyatville

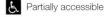 Partially accessible

Braille guide, scented plants, guide dogs allowed

Plant sales Rare Plant Fairs

Other gardens in the area
Belvoir Castle (not NT)
Grimsthorpe Castle (not NT)

Beningbrough Hall

Apr	spring bulbs
May	tulips, cherry trees
Jun	mixed borders
Jul	roses
Aug	lavender
Sep	formal gardens
Oct	apples and pears
Win	closed

Beningbrough, York, YO30 1DD
Tel 01904 470666
Fax 01904 470002
Email
beningbrough@ntrust.org.uk

Location (8:D6) 8ml NW of York,
2ml W of Shipton, 2ml SE of
Linton-on-Ouse (A19)
[105: SE516586]

The planting of the garden is relatively recent but is within a much earlier structure, with old brick walls. Mixed borders of bulbs, shrubs, roses, perennials and annuals and two small formal gardens: a restored Victorian walled kitchen garden, which is managed organically, features huge lavender beds and over 60 local apple and pear varieties; and an American Garden of shrubs and trees from North America. Other features include a liquorice bed, conservatory and wildlife pond. 'Seeds of Beningbrough' wood sculptures in the garden. Wilderness play area. River walks nearby in the 18th-century park.

Soil Silty loam

Terrain Flat

Altitude 50m/164ft

Area 3 hectares/7 acres

Gardeners 4 full-time, 1 seasonal

Partially accessible

Scented plants, guide dogs allowed

Plant sales Spring Plant Fair

Other gardens in the area
Fountains Abbey
Nunnington Hall
Castle Howard (not NT)
Newby Hall (not NT)

The Victorian walled kitchen garden (NTPL/Stephen Robson)

Benthall Hall

Intimate and carefully restored plantsman's garden and kitchen garden. Home of George Maw and his plant collections 1860-90, some plants now naturalised in the grounds. Subsequently the home of Robert Bateman, son of James and Maria Bateman of Biddulph Grange, who were responsible for some of the present garden. The garden was replanted under the guidance of Graham Stuart Thomas.

The Benthall family occupy the house as tenants and have done much, with the support of the National Trust, to maintain the interest and peaceful beauty of this lovely garden.

Apr	spring bulbs, flowering cherries
May	spring fruit trees, crab apples
Jun	roses
Jul	roses, martagon lillies
Aug	herbaceous borders, clematis
Sep	herbaceous fruit, colchicums
Oct	
Win	closed

Broseley, Shropshire TF12 5RX
Tel 01952 882159
Email benthall@ntrust.org.uk

Location (6:C6) 1ml NW of Broseley (B4375), 4ml NE of Much Wenlock, 1ml SW of Ironbridge [127: SJ658025]

The rose garden (NTPL/John Blake)

Soil Alkaline, heavy soil

Terrain Exposed site on hill top with woodland

Altitude 189m/620ft

Area 1.2 hectares/3 acres

Gardeners 1 full-time

Great gardeners Graham Stuart Thomas

 Partially accessible

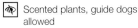 Scented plants, guide dogs allowed

Other gardens in the area
Dudmaston
Moseley Old Hall
Hodnet (not NT)

Berrington Hall

Apr	snowdrops, cyclamen, bluebells, woodland walk
May	wistaria, azaleas, rhododendrons
Jun	wistaria
Jul	roses
Aug	asters, anemones, cottage garden flowers
Sep	asters, anemones, cottage garden flowers
Oct	apples
Win	snowdrops

nr Leominster, Herefordshire
HR6 0DW
Tel 01568 615721
Fax 01568 613263
Email berrington@ntrust.org.uk

Location (6:B8) 3ml N of Leominster, 7ml S of Ludlow on W side of A49 [137: SO510637]

Soil Clay/silty loam

Terrain Mostly level, surrounded by hills

Altitude 76-137m/249-449ft

Area 4.6 hectares/11 acres

Gardeners 2 full-time

Great gardeners Capability Brown

 Fully accessible

Scented plants, guide dogs allowed

Events Spring Plant Fair, May, Estate guided walks & Apple Week

Other gardens in the area
Burford House (not NT)
Hampton Court (not NT)
Stockton Bury (not NT)

The fine gardens directly around the mansion were first developed by the 6th Lord Rodney and his wife Sarah in the 1840s, in accordance with mid-19th-century fashion for laurel walks and specimen trees and plants. Around 1900 the 1st Lord Cawley bought the estate and planted the avenue of golden yews which leads the visitor from the Triumphal Arch to the mansion. A wonderful walled garden to the right of this path contains the National Collection of Historic Hereford and Marches Apples, many of which are no longer in general cultivation. In May an ancient and glorious wistaria blooms here. There are many beautiful azaleas and rhododendrons in the Woodland Walk, planted by the 3rd Lord Cawley; and other unusual plants and trees including a rare yellow-flowered marrow (*Thladiantha oliveri*). Berrington Hall is set in a splendid 18th-century landscape designed by Capability Brown.

Old apple varieties from the National Collection
(NTPL/Stephen Robson)

Opposite: 'China' looking towards the temple (NTPL/Ian Shaw)

Biddulph Grange Garden

One of Britain's most exciting and unusual Victorian gardens, created in the mid-19th century by James and Maria Bateman with Edward Cooke the marine painter. A series of connected compartments designed by the Batemans to display specimens from their wide-ranging plant collection. Visitors are taken on a miniature tour of the world, including China, Egypt and a Scottish glen, as well as a rhododendron garden and, since 2001, an ice-house and fountain in Mrs Bateman's garden. The highly accurate restoration was made possible from drawings, early photographs and descriptions, resulting in the most complete high-Victorian garden in Britain.

Apr	spring bedding
May	rhododendrons, peonies
Jun	lilies, herbaceous
Jul	summer bedding, giant lilies
Aug	bedding, dahlias
Sep	dahlias, fuchsias
Oct	autumn colour
Win	closed

Biddulph Grange, Biddulph,
Stoke-on-Trent, Staffordshire
ST8 7SD
Tel 01782 517999
Fax 01782 510624
Email
biddulphgrange@ntrust.org.uk

Location (6:D4) ½ml N of
Biddulph, 3½ml SE of Congleton,
7ml N of Stoke-on-Trent. Access
from A527 (Tunstall–Congleton
road). Entrance on Grange Road
[118: SJ895591]

Soil Acid

Terrain Steps, narrow rocky
pathways

Altitude 150m/492ft

Area 6 hectares/15 acres

Gardeners 5 full-time, 2 part-time

Great gardeners James & Maria
Bateman

Partially accessible

Braille guide, scented
plants, guide dogs allowed

Other gardens in the area
Dunham Massey
Hare Hill
Little Moreton Hall
Lyme Park
Tatton Park
Bridgemere Garden World (not NT)
Dorothy Clive Garden (not NT)
Stapely Water Garden (not NT)

Blickling Hall

Apr	daffodils
May	bluebells
Jun	herbaceous borders
Jul	herbaceous borders
Aug	herbaceous borders
Sep	herbaceous borders
Oct	penstemons
Win	snowdrops

Blickling, Norwich, NR11 6NF
Tel 01263 738030
Fax 01263 731660
Email blickling@ntrust.org.uk

Location (4:J2) 1½ml NW of
Aylsham on B1354. Signposted
off A140 Norwich (15ml S) to
Cromer (10ml N) road
[133: TG178286]

Soil Slightly acidic

Terrain Flat with some
undulations

Altitude 300m/984ft

Area 17.4 hectares/43 acres

Gardeners 5 full-time,
3 seasonal

Great gardeners W. A. Nesfield,
Norah Lindsay

 Fully accessible

Braille guide, scented
plants, guide dogs allowed

Plant sales March–Oct

Events Garden talks

Other gardens in the area
Felbrigg Hall
Mannington Hall (not NT)
Wolterton Hall (not NT)

Delightful gardens and 18th-century landscape park surrounding the Jacobean house, offering colour and variety throughout the year, from spring bulbs, magnolias, azaleas, rhododendrons and herbaceous flower parterre to magnificent autumn colour. Victorian sunken garden, remodelled in the 1930s by Norah Lindsay, consisting of four colourful herbaceous beds and yew topiary around a 17th-century fountain. A path leads from the parterre to a Doric temple, commissioned by the 1st Earl of Buckinghamshire, probably in the 1730s. The late 18th-century orangery, on the border of the park and garden, houses camellias and ferns. Formal wilderness garden with radial walks lined by avenues of Turkey oak, lime and beech. The northern wilderness area hides a charming secret garden with summer-house, sundial and scented plants. Beyond the garden lies the wooded 18th-century landscape park planted with oak, beech and sweet chestnuts and featuring a long man-made lake, offering miles of attractive lakeside and parkland walks.

The Doric temple and parterre
(NTPL/Nick Meers)

Bodnant

One of the world's most spectacular gardens, situated above the River Conwy with stunning views across Snowdonia. Begun in 1875, Bodnant is the creation of four generations of Aberconways and features huge Italianate terraces and formal lawns on its upper level, with wooded valley, stream and wild garden below. Dramatic colours throughout the season, with notable collections of rhododendrons, magnolias and camellias and the spectacular laburnum arch, a 55-metre tunnel of golden blooms, in mid-May and early June. Bodnant hosts the National Collections of *Embothriums, Eucryphia, Magnolia* and *Rhododendron forestii*.

Note: The garden and refreshment pavilion are managed by Lord Aberconway, VMH.

Apr	magnolias, camellias
May	rhododendrons, laburnum arch
Jun	herbaceous borders
Jul	roses, water lilies
Aug	hydrangeas. eucryphia
Sep	autumn colour
Oct	autumn colour
Win	closed

Tal-y-Cafn, Colwyn Bay, Conwy LL28 5RE
Tel 01492 650460
Fax 01492 650448

Location (0:F2) 8ml S of Llandudno and Colwyn Bay off A470, entrance ½ml along the Eglwysbach road. Signposted from A55 [115/116: SH801723]

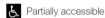
Soil Stiff boulder clay, overlaying friable shaly rock

Terrain Mainly sloping, steep in places

Altitude 65m/213ft

Area 32 hectares/79 acres

Gardeners 20 full-time

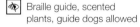 Partially accessible

Braille guide, scented plants, guide dogs allowed

Other gardens in the area
Bodelwyddan Castle (not NT)
Portmeirion Village and Gardens (not NT)

The laburnum arch
(NTPL/Christopher Gallagher)

Buckland Abbey

Apr	camellias, rhododendrons
May	azaleas, magnolias
Jun	herb garden
Jul	herb garden
Aug	herbaceous plants
Sep	magnolias
Oct	autumn colour
Win	scented shrubs

Yelverton, Devon PL20 6EY
Tel 01822 853607
Fax 01822 855448
Email
bucklandabbey@ntrust.org.uk

Location (1:F8) 6ml S of
Tavistock, 11ml N of Plymouth:
turn off A386 ¼ml S of Yelverton
[201: SX487667]

Soil Acid loam on shale

Terrain Steep

Altitude 75m/246ft

Area 1.2 hectares/3 acres

Gardeners 1 full-time, 1 part-time

Great gardeners Vita Sackville-
West

 Partially accessible

 Scented plants, guide dogs
allowed

Other gardens in the area
Antony
Cotehele
Lydford Gorge
Saltram
The Garden House, Buckland
    Monachorum (not NT)

An interesting herb garden, inspired by Vita Sackville-West, with a series of box-edged beds, filled with herbs and medicinal plants. On the north-east side of the Abbey where once stood an ancient row of yew trees, is a newly-created Elizabethan-style garden with topiary and old varieties of fruit trees. Standing on the south side of the Abbey are two magnificent large evergreen magnolias, *M. grandiflora* and *M. delavayi*, which flower right through until the first frosts. Shrubs and herbaceous borders.

Detail of the herb garden
(NTPL/Andrew Butler)

Buscot Park

The garden and park were created in the late 18th century, with a deer park and massive walled garden. In the 20th century Harold Peto constructed the famous water garden. The walled garden has been replanted, with a pleached hornbeam avenue and purple-flowered Judas tunnel leading to a central fountain pond, with surrounding seasonal borders. Peter Coats planted an attractive double border in the 1980s. Statuary and large variety of tree planting.

Apr	all season interest
May	all season interest
Jun	all season interest
Jul	all season interest
Aug	all season interest
Sep	all season interest
Oct	closed
Win	closed

Estate Office, Buscot Park,
Faringdon, Oxfordshire SN7 8BU
Tel 01367 240786
Fax 01367 241794
Email estbuscot@aol.com

Location (2:B4) Between
Lechlade and Faringdon, on
A417 [163: SU239973]

Soil London clay

Terrain Hilly

Altitude 200m/656ft

Area 28 hectares/69 acres

Gardeners 3 full-time, 1 part-time, 1 seasonal

Great gardeners Harold Peto,
Peter Coats

 Partially accessible

 Guide dogs allowed

Other gardens in the area
Kelmscott Manor (not NT)

Harold Peto's water garden
(NTPL/Vera Collingwood)

Calke Abbey

Apr	
May	spring bedding, auriculas
Jun	
Jul	summer bedding
Aug	herbaceous borders
Sep	vegetables
Oct	
Win	closed

Ticknall, Derby, Derbyshire
DE73 1LE
Tel 01332 863822
Fax 01332 865272
Email calkeabbey@ntrust.org.uk

Location (5:B7) 10ml S of Derby,
on A514 at Ticknall between
Swadlincote and Melbourne.
Access from M42/A42 Jn 13 and
A50 Derby South
[128: SK356239]

The early 18th-century mansion is surrounded by informal pleasure grounds, laid out by Sir Harry Harpur and his son, Sir Henry, between about 1770 and 1820. The extensive walled gardens are being sympathetically restored by the NT. The flower garden has formal bedding in bold contrasting colours. The physic garden provides a wide range of fruit and vegetables, including many old varieties. Key architectural features include the partially restored orangery, the famous – and unique – 18th-century auricula theatre, extensive glasshouses and the gardener's bothy. Beyond the walled gardens, the pleasure gardens have been fenced to exclude deer and allow replanting of shrubs and trees.

Soil Medium loam

Terrain Undulating pleasure grounds, level walled garden

Altitude 120m/394ft

Area 4 hectares/10 acres

Gardeners 2+1 apprentice full-time, 1 seasonal

 Partially accessible

Scented plants, guide dogs allowed

Plant sales spring and autumn. Kitchen Garden produce for sale

Events Guided walks, Art in the Garden, Opera in the Garden, Apple Day

Other gardens in the area Kedleston Hall Melbourne Hall (not NT)

The walled flower garden
(NTPL/Nick Meers)

Canons Ashby

Formal garden created between 1708 and 1717 by Edward Dryden. Recognised as one of the best surviving formal layouts in the style of George London and Henry Wise, and a considerable influence on the Lutyens-Gertrude Jekyll generation of gardeners. Derelict and overgrown when rescued by the NT, the restoration work of the 1980s is maturing. The garden is divided by stone walls and yew hedges into courts with terraces and topiary. Early 18th-century timber gates and garden seats together with fine Cedar of Lebanon. In the Green Court is a lead statue of a shepherd boy attributed to Jan van Nost (early 18th century). Old fruit varieties including plums, pears and apples of the same varieties as found in the *Mary Rose*. Terracing, mixed rose and herbaceous borders, mulberry border. Culinary and medicinal herb border.

Apr	bulbs
May	camassias, fruit blossom
Jun	herb border
Jul	roses, topiary
Aug	mixed climbers
Sep	herbaceous borders, climbers
Oct	topiary, fruit
Win	closed

Canons Ashby, Daventry, Northamptonshire NN11 3SD
Tel 01327 860044
Fax 01327 860168
Email canonsashby@ntrust.org.uk

Location (5:C9) Easy access from either M40, exit 11 or M1, exit 16. From M1, take A45 (Daventry) and at Weedon crossroads turn left onto A5; 3ml S turn right onto unclassified road through Litchborough. From M40 at Banbury, take A422 (Buckingham) and after 2ml turn left onto B4525; after 3ml turn left onto unclassified road signposted to property [152: SP577506]

Soil Neutral, medium to light

Terrain Gentle slope, exposed and windy site

Altitude 150m/492ft

Area 1.3 hectares/3 acres

Gardeners 1 full-time, 1 part-time

 Partially accessible

Braille guide, scented plants, guide dogs allowed

Plant sales Plant fair

Events Paint the Garden, guided walks

Other gardens in the area
Farnborough Hall
Stowe Landscape Garden
Upton House
National Herb Centre (not NT)

18th-century statue of a shepherd boy in the Green Court (NTPL/Andrew Butler)

Castle Drogo

Apr	spring bulbs, rhododendrons, magnolia
May	spring bulbs, rhododendrons, magnolia
Jun	roses, herbaceous borders
Jul	roses, herbaceous borders
Aug	roses, herbaceous borders
Sep	shrubs
Oct	autumn colour
Win	architectural features

Drewsteignton, nr Exeter, Devon
EX6 6PB
Tel 01647 433306
Fax 01647 433186
Email castledrogo@ntrust.org.uk

Location (1:G7) 5ml S of A30
Exeter–Okehampton road via
Crockernwell or A382
Moretonhampstead–Whiddon
Down road; coaches must use
the latter and turn off at Sandy
Park [191: SX721900]

Soil Acid 5.5-6.0pH fine loam to
fine silt and stone

Terrain Rocky outcrop

Altitude 263m/863ft

Area 4.8 hectares/12 acres

Gardeners 2 full-time, 1 seasonal

Great gardeners Edwin Lutyens,
George Dillistone

 Fully accessible

 Braille guide, scented
plants, guide dogs allowed

Plant sales Plant fairs

Events Full programme, please
telephone for details

Other gardens in the area
The Mythic Garden (not NT)

This 20th-century Norman fantasy castle, high on
Dartmoor, was designed by Sir Edwin Lutyens for
Julius Drewe, founder of the Home and Colonial
Stores. The main flower gardens, with architectural yew
hedges, are beyond the drive, to the north-east. On the
terrace above is a wonderfully imaginative herbaceous
garden: the paths form an Indian motif and the
plantings among them are of varied colour and
texture. There are also rhododendron and fragrant
gardens, the whole design linked by hedges, paths,
vistas, walls and domes.

The herbaceous garden
(NTPL/Neil Campbell-Sharp)

Castle Ward

The 1st Lord Bangor and his wife Anne had very different views on style – he favoured classical, she Gothick. Their house, built in the 1760s, was a mixture of both, but Lord Bangor got his way with the surrounding landscape. He incorporated into his scheme some earlier features, such as the yew terraces, three walks planted with English yews, and Temple Water, an early 18th-century canal-shaped lake, one of the few remaining features of its kind in Ireland. The sunken parterre garden, created by the Ward family in the 19th century, features a marble statue of Neptune standing in a circular pool. With views over Strangford Lough, Castle Ward offers extensive walks in mixed woodland and throughout the estate.

Apr	daffodils
May	bluebells, rhododendrons,
Jun	herbaceous borders
Jul	roses
Aug	sunken garden
Sep	funghi
Oct	autumn colour
Win	snowdrops

Strangford, Downpatrick, Down
BT30 7LS
Tel 028 4488 1204
Fax 028 4488 1729
Email castleward@ntrust.org.uk

Location (1:K6) 7ml NE of Downpatrick, 1½ml W of Strangford village on A25, on S shore of Strangford Lough, entrance by Ballyculter Lodge [J752494]

Soil Well-drained loam/gravel, neutral

Terrain Rocky, hilly, rolling down to lough

Altitude 0–400m/1312ft

Area 250 hectares/618 acres

Gardeners 1 full-time, 3 volunteer part-time

Partially accessible

 Scented plants, guide dogs allowed

Events Regular guided woodland and estate walks

Other gardens in the area
Mount Stewart
Rowallane
Castlewellan Arboretum (not NT)

The sunken parterre garden
(NTPL/Matthew Antrobus)

Charlecote Park

Apr	parterre, spring display
May	wistaria, parterre
Jun	herbaceous border
Jul	herbaceous border, parterre
Aug	summer display
Sep	summer display
Oct	woodland garden
Win	woodland garden

Warwick, Warwickshire
CV35 9ER
Tel 01789 470277
Fax 01789 470544
Email
charlecotepark@ntrust.org.uk

Location (6:E8) 1ml W of
Wellesbourne, 5ml E of Stratford-
upon-Avon, 6ml S of Warwick on
N side of B4086
[151: SP263564]

Soil Light, sandy

Terrain Flat

Altitude 50m/164ft

Area 2 hectares/5 acres

Gardeners 2 full-time

Great gardeners Capability
Brown

Fully accessible

Guide dogs allowed

Plant sales May

Other gardens in the area
Baddesley Clinton
Coughton Court
Farnborough Hall
Hidcote Manor
Packwood House
Upton House
Kiftsgate Court (not NT)

Relatively small gardens, but surrounded by a Capability
Brown landscape park which is overlooked by the
formal garden. The new Green Court garden in front
of the house was designed by Sir Edmund Fairfax-
Lucy in 1999, and contains box, yew and ornamental
fruit trees as well as statues of a shepherd and
shepherdess. Restored parterre with design taken from
the original Victorian parterre. The wild garden was
redesigned in 1995 with a small water feature, shrubs,
grasses and seasonal flowers. The herbaceous border
was moved and replanted 2000/2001. There is a 19th-
century orangery and a summer-house by the Cedar
Lawn. A border close to the Orangery has been planted
with species mentioned in his plays by Shakespeare,
who is said to have poached deer in the park.

Croquet lawn can be used by the public thoughout
the season.

Early 18th-century statues in the forecourt
(NTPL/Matthew Antrobus)

Chartwell

The garden planned by Sir Winston and Lady Churchill, with terraced lawns, ponds, orchard and flower borders, in a pleasant country-house garden style, enjoying fine views over the Weald of Kent. The ornamental design and planting reflect the taste of Lady Churchill, especially the walled rose garden. Lovely water garden with white foxgloves. In 1958 a golden rose walk was created by their children to commemorate the Churchills' golden wedding.

Apr	daffodils, camellias, magnolias
May	rhododendrons
Jun	sweet peas
Jul	roses, sweet peas
Aug	roses, eucryphia
Sep	dahlias
Oct	dahlias
Win	closed

Westerham, Kent TN16 1PS
Tel 01732 868381
Fax 01732 868193
Email chartwell@ntrust.org.uk

Location (2:G6) 2ml S of Westerham, fork left off B2026 after 1½ml [188: TQ455515]

Soil Medium loam over greensand

Terrain Hill-top garden dipping into valley

Altitude 120m/394ft

Area 33 hectares/82 acres

Gardeners 5 full-time

♿ Partially accessible

Braille guide, scented plants, guide dogs allowed

🐕 dogs allowed on leads

Other gardens in the area
Emmetts Garden
Ightham Mote

Statue of Sir Winston and Lady Churchill by Oscar Nemon
(NTPL/David Sellman)

41

Chastleton

Apr	interest all season
May	interest all season
Jun	interest all season
Jul	interest all season
Aug	interest all season
Sep	interest all season
Oct	interest all season
Win	closed

Chastleton, Moreton-in-Marsh,
Oxfordshire GL56 0SU
Tel/Fax 01608 674355
Email chastleton@ntrust.org.uk

Location (2:B3) 6ml from Stow-
on-the-Wold. Approach only
from A436 between the A44
(west of Chipping Norton) and
Stow [163: SP248291]

Soil Light loam (stony)

Terrain Mainly level

Altitude 180m/591ft

Area 2.4 hectares/6 acres

Gardeners 2 part-time

 Partially accessible

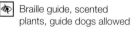 Braille guide, scented
plants, guide dogs allowed

Other gardens in the area
Hidcote Manor
Snowshill Manor
Stowe Landscape Garden
Upton House

Chastleton House has remained remarkably unchanged since its construction *c.*1612. The surrounding garden is claimed to be of the same date and so is potentially an even rarer survival, although archives show that it was at least partially replanted in 1828 in an early instance of garden restoration work. The apparently low level of gardening here is intentional; the approach of the Trust is to repair rather than restore, although some beds have been replanted and lawns relaid. But the policy of contrived neglect – actually requiring as much planning and management as more conventional gardening – has helped to retain the property's unique atmosphere of slumbering peace.

Circle of box topiary (NTPL/Rupert Truman)

Opposite: Bronze nymph emerging from the pool garden (NTPL/David Hall)

Chirk Castle

A family garden that has been changed over the years according to fashion and to the enthusiasm of the owners. Much of the formal 17th- and early 18th-century garden was swept away by William Emes in the 1760s. Today the garden has several different areas: a formal garden with topiary, small herbaceous border and rose garden; shrub garden with herbaceous beds and rare shrubs; rhododendrons, azaleas and hydrangeas; a fine larch and *Davidia involucrata* (Handkerchief tree). There is also a small pond with fish and Emperor dragonflies. The hawk house that once housed Lord Howard de Walden's birds now provides shelter from the elements for visitors. Behind the hawk house lies the rockery with many alpine and sun-loving plants. A terrace leads to a pavilion by Emes and also the lime tree avenue.

While this garden is finest in spring, there is much summer interest, in particular a fine rockery.

Apr	osmanthus, aubretias, bulbs
May	bulbs, rhododendrons, magnolias, cornus
Jun	azaleas, cornus, shrubs, iris
Jul	herbaceous border, roses, rockery
Aug	hydrangeas, roses, rockery
Sep	topiary, rockery, herbaceous border, roses
Oct	acers, herbaceous border, topiary
Win	shrubs, snowdrops, rhododendrons

Chirk, Wrexham, Wrexham
LL14 5AF
Tel 01691 777701
Fax 01691 774706
Email chirkcastle@ntrust.org.uk

Location (0:H3) Entrance 1ml off A5, 2ml W of Chirk village; 7ml S of Wrexham, signposted off A483 [126:SJ275388]

Soil Sandy loam

Terrain Gently sloping south-east

Altitude 213m/699ft

Area 2.2 hectares/5 acres

Gardeners 3 full-time

Great gardeners William Emes, Norah Lindsay

Partially accessible

Scented plants, guide dogs allowed

Other gardens in the area
Erddig
Powis Castle

Clandon Park

Apr	daffodil meadow
May	herbaceous border
Jun	herbaceous border
Jul	herbaceous border, Dutch garden
Aug	herbaceous border, Dutch garden
Sep	
Oct	beech autumn colour
Win	

West Clandon, Guildford, Surrey
GU4 7RQ
Tel 01483 222482
Fax 01483 223479
Email clandonpark@ntrust.org.uk

Location (2:F6) At West Clandon
on A247, 3ml E of Guildford; if
using A3 follow signposts to
Ripley to join A247 via B2215
[186: TQ042512]

Soil Alkaline

Terrain Level, reasonably
sheltered

Altitude 88m/289ft

Area 3 hectares/7 acres

Gardeners 1 full-time

 Fully accessible

 Braille guide, scented
plants, guide dogs allowed

Events Easter egg hunt, Easter
Monday

Other gardens in the area
Claremont
Ham House
Hatchlands Park
Nymans
Winkworth Arboretum
Wisley RHS Garden (not NT)

These attractive gardens, surrounding the grand
Palladian mansion built *c*.1730, feature a south-facing
parterre with seasonal bedding arrangements, pleached
hornbeams and seats. A grassy bank leads towards the
grotto (unfortunately closed to visitors) and a stunning
copper beech. The lawn is bordered by herbaceous
borders and a pollarded lime path leads to the church
and a sunken Dutch garden filled with plants chosen
for their scent. A central water feature makes this a
pleasant and meditative spot. The gardens also contain a
Maori Meeting House with a fascinating history.

Left: Detail from the Maori hut
(NTPL/Nick Meers)

Below: The parterre, with the roof
of the Maori hut in the middle
distance (NTPL/Nick Meers)

Claremont

Claremont's creation and development involved some of the great names in garden history: Sir John Vanbrugh, Charles Bridgeman, William Kent and Capability Brown all played their part in the landscape seen today. The garden, begun *c.*1715, was described in 1726 by Stephen Switzer as 'the noblest of any in Europe'. The many features include a lake island with pavilion, grotto, turf amphitheatre and camellia terrace. Lovely walks with ever-changing vistas.

Note: No coaches admitted on Sundays or bank holidays.

Across the lake towards the amphitheatre (NTPL/Ian Shaw)

Apr	tree heathers
May	deciduous azaleas
Jun	rhododendron ponticum
Jul	
Aug	
Sep	
Oct	
Win	camellias

Portsmouth Road, Esher, Surrey
KT10 9JG
Tel 01372 467806
Fax 01372 464394
Email claremont@ntrust.org.uk

Location (2:F6) On S edge of Esher, on E side of A307 (no access from Esher bypass) [187: TQ128634]

Soil Sandy loam

Terrain Undulating

Altitude 30m/98ft

Area 20 hectares/49 acres

Gardeners 2 full-time, 1 part-time

Great gardeners Charles Bridgeman, Sir John Vanbrugh, William Kent, Capability Brown

 Partially accessible

Braille guide, scented plants, guide dogs allowed

Events Plant Fair mid-May, guided walks April to Nov, mid-July themed evenings of music and fireworks, phone for details

Other gardens in the area
Ham House
Polesden Lacey
Hampton Court (not NT)
Painshill Park (not NT)
Wisley RHS Garden (not NT)

Clevedon Court

Apr	
May	Judas tree, arbutus, drimys, choisya, dipelta
Jun	catalpa, ceanothus
Jul	canna lilies, tilia
Aug	tulip trees, eucryphia, canna lillies, cardoons, fuchsias
Sep	fuchsias, hypericum, canna lillies
Oct	closed
Win	closed

The garden of 14th-century Clevedon Court rises behind the house on three terraces. Originally these south-facing terraces had espaliered fruit trees but are now planted with tender species such as the Judas tree, strawberry tree, *Canna iridiflora*, palm, myrtle, fuchsias and splendid magnolias. A summer-house on one of the terraces counterbalances an 18th-century garden house on the other. Wooded areas of ilex above the terraces.

Tickenham Road, Clevedon, Somerset BS21 6QU
Tel 01275 872257

Location (1:J4) 1½ml E of Clevedon, on Bristol road (B3130), signposted from M5 exit 20 [172: ST423716]

Soil Lime loam

Terrain Hillside

Altitude 30m/98ft

Area 10 hectares/25 acres

Gardeners 1 full-time, 1 part-time

♿ Partially accessible

Scented plants, guide dogs allowed

Other gardens in the area
Dyrham Park

Detail of a canna lily
(NTPL/Mark Bolton)

46

Cliveden

Large 18th-century landscape magnificently sited high on an escarpment overlooking the Thames Valley. Contains a sequence of historical garden styles: early amphitheatre of 1732 and avenues and rides by Charles Bridgeman; temple and pavilion by Giacomo Leoni; parterre in 18th-century French style; Long Garden with topiary and hedges of 1900; wall shrubs, herbaceous borders in Gertrude Jekyll style; water garden in Eastern style from 1900; Secret Garden designed by Sir Geoffrey Jellicoe in 1959, now planted with grasses and herbaceous perennials. Fountains, sculpture and statuary mostly introduced by the Astor family from 1894. 'Hanging Woods' under restoration. Woodland walks and river frontage.

Apr	spring bulbs
May	blossom, magnolias, rhododendrons
Jun	herbaceous borders
Jul	herbaceous borders
Aug	herbaceous borders
Sep	autumn colour
Oct	autumn colour
Win	spring bulbs, shrubs

Taplow, Maidenhead,
Buckinghamshire SL6 0JA
Tel 01628 605069
Fax 01628 669461
Email cliveden@ntrust.org.uk

Location (2:E5) 2ml N of Taplow; leave M4 at exit 7 onto A4, or M40 at exit 4 onto A404 to Marlow and follow town signs. Entrance by main gates opposite Feathers Inn [175: SU915851]

Chinese pagoda in the water garden (NTPL/Ian Shaw)

Soil Gravel overlaying chalk with clay seams

Terrain Hill-top and escarpment

Altitude 75m/246ft

Area 73 hectares/180 acres

Gardeners 10 full-time

Great gardeners Charles Bridgeman, John Fleming, Norah Lindsay, Geoffrey Jellicoe, Graham Stuart Thomas

 Partially accessible

Braille guide, scented plants, guide dogs allowed

Plant sales Autumn Plant Fair

Events Guided walks, woodland walks, open-air theatre, Opera in the Garden, art class, craft fair

Other gardens in the area
Greys Court
Osterley Park
Stowe Landscape Garden
Waddesdon Manor
Hampton Court (not NT)
Savill Garden (not NT)

Clumber Park

Apr	tree blossom
May	rhododendrons
Jun	delphiniums, iris, peonies
Jul	herbaceous borders
Aug	herbaceous borders
Sep	kitchen garden produce, herbaceous borders
Oct	apples, autumn colour
Win	spring bulbs

The Estate Office, Clumber Park,
Worksop, Nottinghamshire
S80 3AZ
Tel 01909 476592
Fax 01909 500721

Location (5:C5) 4½ml SE of
Worksop, 6½ml SW of Retford,
1ml from A1/A57, 11ml from M1
exit 30
[120: SK645774 or 120: SK6267
46]

Soil Sandy loam

Terrain Undulating

Altitude 30m/98ft

Area 10 hectares/25 acres

Gardeners 3 full-time, 1 part-time, 2 seasonal

Partially accessible

Scented plants, guide dogs allowed

Plant sales Spring and autumn

Events Clumber Country Show,
Clumber Horticultural Show,
vegetable/fruit tasting and
apple/grape selling days, guided
garden and pleasure ground
walks/tours

A late 18th-century pleasure ground and a partially restored walled kitchen garden. The gardens are at the centre of an extensive estate that belonged to the Dukes of Newcastle. The estate is virtually intact apart from the mansion and formal gardens, which were dismantled in the late 1930s. The pleasure ground, under restoration, comprises the remains of the formal features, picturesque walks, beautiful specimen trees and garden temples on the north bank of a 32-hectare artificial lake. The working kitchen garden is managed organically and produces a wide variety of fruit, vegetables and cut flowers, which are available for sale in season. Of particular interest is the fully-restored Long Range (135 metres of continuous Edwardian glasshouses) containing fig house, vineries, palm house, a display house, three peach houses and orchard house. Striking double herbaceous borders and working beehives. Tool exhibition and garden museum.

Other gardens in the area

Belton House
Gunby Hall
Hardwick Hall
Nostell Priory

Brodsworth Hall (not NT)
Hodsock Priory (not NT)
Newstead Abbey (not NT)
Rufford Park (not NT)

Tomatoes growing in one of the
Edwardian glasshouses
(NTPL/Stephen Robson)

Colby Woodland Garden

Secluded woodland setting with one of the finest collections of rhododendrons and azaleas in Wales. Noted for its bluebells and spectacular autumn colour. Good summer interest from hydrangeas, herbaceous borders, specimen trees and shrubs. Walled garden, gothic-style gazebo and water feature.

Apr	camellias, bluebells
May	rhododendrons and azaleas
Jun	rhododendrons and azaleas
Jul	hydrangeas
Aug	hydrangeas
Sep	autumn colour
Oct	autumn colour
Win	closed

Soil Clay/acid

Terrain Gently sloping valley

Altitude 100m/328ft

Area 20 hectares/49 acres

Gardeners 2 full-time

Partially accessible

Braille guide, scented plants, guide dogs allowed

dogs on leads, not in walled garden

Plant sales May, June and September

Events Children's fun days, Easter Egg Trail, guided walks with gardener in charge (phone for dates and events leaflet)

Other gardens in the area
Botanical Gardens of Wales (not NT)

Amroth, Narberth, Pembrokeshire SA67 8PP
Tel/Fax 01834 811885

Location (0:D9) 1½ml inland from Amroth beside Carmarthen Bay. Follow brown signs from A477 Tenby–Carmarthen road or off coast road at Amroth Castle [158: SN155080]

Rhododendrons in the woodland garden (NTPL/Andrew Butler)

Coleton Fishacre

Apr	valley garden
May	valley garden
Jun	terrace borders, valley garden
Jul	terrace borders, walled garden
Aug	terrace borders, walled garden
Sep	terrace borders, walled garden
Oct	terrace borders, walled garden
Win	closed

This valley garden, developed by Rupert and Lady Dorothy D'Oyly Carte in the 1920s, has a spectacular setting on a beautiful stretch of NT-owned coast. In the spring and early summer, wild flowers mingle with rhododendrons, camellias and azaleas planted amongst the collection of tender and exotic plants that thrive in the subtropical climate and sheltered location. The formal terraces and walled garden provide summer-long interest. Paths descend the wooded valley weaving along the contours and through quiet glades past tranquil ponds to a small cove under the cliffs.

Coleton, Kingswear, Dartmouth, Devon TQ6 0EQ
Tel 01803 752466
Fax 01803 753017
Email coletonfishacre@ntrust.org.uk

Location (1:G8) 3ml from Kingswear; take Lower Ferry road, turn off at toll house (take care on narrow lanes near property) [202: SX910508]

Soil Acid

Terrain Valley garden, coastal

Altitude 30-100m/98-328ft

Area 9.5 hectares/23 acres

Gardeners 3 full-time, 1 part-time

 Partially accessible

Braille guide, scented plants, guide dogs allowed

Plant sales At reception

Events Guided walks May and September, Midsummer garden picnic and garden stroll

Other gardens in the area
Compton Castle
Greenway
Killerton
Overbecks
Saltram
Dartington Hall Gardens (not NT)
Torbay Plant World (not NT)

Detail of the rill garden
(NTPL/Stephen Robson)

Compton Castle

Set in the glorious Devon countryside on the outskirts of Torbay. Much work has been invested in the construction of the stone-pillared pergola, built using authentic materials. A range of traditional fragrant climbing roses has been planted, complementing those in the rose garden. Varieties include Paul's Lemon Pillar, Constance Spry, William Lobb and Parkdirektor Riggers.

Apr	
May	water lilies
Jun	roses, water lilies
Jul	roses
Aug	
Sep	
Oct	
Win	closed

Soil Acid, silty clay

Terrain Lush valley

Altitude 65-70m/213-230ft

Area 1.3 hectares/3 acres

Gardeners 1 part-time, 1 seasonal

 Partially accessible, (limited access)

 (on lead in car park)

Events Occasional concerts and outdoor plays

Other gardens in the area
Coleton Fishacre
Greenway
Dartington Hall (not NT)
Torbay Plant World (not NT)

Marldon, Paignton, Devon
TQ3 1TA
Tel 01803 875740
(answerphone)
Fax 01803 875740

Location (1:G8) At Compton, 3ml W of Torquay, 1ml N of Marldon; from the Newton Abbot–Totnes road (A381) turn left at Ipplepen crossroads and W off Torbay ring road via Marldon [202: SX865648]

P 🚹 🚻

The lily pond (NT)

Cotehele

Apr	daffodils
May	rhododendrons
Jun	herbaceous borders
Jul	herbaceous borders, cut flower garden
Aug	cut flower garden
Sep	pumpkins and apples
Oct	autumn colour
Win	Christmas garland, evergreens, daffodils

The garden at Cotehele provides an atmospheric and romantic setting for the ancient house, hidden in the heart of the Tamar Valley. Surrounding the house are a series of formal gardens, terraces, yew hedges, an orchard and a daffodil meadow. Below, the sheltered valley garden, containing exotic and tender plants, drops steeply towards the Tamar. Fragments of Cotehele's long history are to be found everywhere, including a medieval stewpond and domed dovecote in the valley, and the 18th-century Prospect Tower on the hill above.

St Dominick, nr Saltash,
Cornwall PL12 6TA
Tel 01579 351346
Fax 01579 351222
Email cotehele@ntrust.org.uk

Location (1:E8) On W bank of the Tamar, 1ml W of Calstock by steep footpath (6ml by road). Calstock can be reached from Plymouth by water (contact Plymouth Boat Cruises Ltd, tel. 01752 822797) and from Calstock (tel. 01822 833331) [201: SX422685]

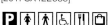

Soil Acid, free draining

Terrain Valley, with flat area around house

Altitude 20m/66ft

Area 5.6 hectares/14 acres

Gardeners 3 full-time,
1 seasonal

 Partially accessible

 Guide dogs allowed

Plant sales Daily

Events Daffodil Exhibition, Apple and Pumpkin Day, Christmas Garland

Other gardens in the area
Antony
Lanhydrock
Saltram
Endsleigh (not NT)
The Garden House (not NT)

The dovecote in the valley garden (NTPL/Stephen Robson)

The Courts

Sir George Hastings occupied the house from 1900 to 1911 and planted yew hedges as a background for his collection of stone statuary. From 1920 Lady Cecilie Goff, influenced by Gertrude Jekyll and Lawrence Johnston, created the garden around this basic structure. The result are formal gardens divided by yew hedges, shrub borders and raised terraces. Many interesting plants and imaginative colour schemes. Features include a conservatory, lily pond, mixed borders and pleached limes. In 1952 an arboretum was created and under-planted with spring bulbs.

Apr	bulbs
May	tulips, hostas, iris
Jun	roses, peonies, achillea
Jul	herbaceous borders, salvia, delphiniums
Aug	herbaceous borders
Sep	orchard, euonymus
Oct	fruits
Win	snowdrops, hellebores

Holt, nr Trowbridge, Wiltshire
BA14 6RR
Tel/Fax 01225 782340
Email courtsgarden@ntrust.org.uk

Soil Alkaline, heavy soil.

Terrain Flat, sheltered enclosed garden

Altitude 61m/200ft

Area 2.8 hectares/7 acres

Gardeners 2 full-time, 1 seasonal

Plant sales Surplus plants when available

Events Walks each month

Other gardens in the area
Lacock Abbey
Stourhead
Iford Manor (not NT)

Location (1:K4) 3ml SW of Melksham, 2½ml E of Bradford-on-Avon, on S side of B3107 [173: ST861618]

 Partially accessible

Braille guide, scented plants, guide dogs allowed

The rill and lily pond (NTPL/Stephen Robson)

Cragside

Apr	spring bulbs
May	tulips, spring bedding, azaleas
Jun	rhododendrons
Jul	carpet bedding, bedding
Aug	carpet bedding, bedding
Sep	dahlia walk
Oct	orchard house fruit
Win	conifers, pinetum

Rothbury, Morpeth,
Northumberland NE65 7PX
Tel 01669 620333/620150
Fax 01669 620066
Email cragside@ntrust.org.uk

Location (9:J5) 13ml SW of
Alnwick (B6341) and 15ml NW of
Morpeth on Wooler road (A697),
turn left on to B6341 at
Moorhouse Crossroads,
entrance 1ml N of Rothbury;
public transport passengers
enter by Reivers Well Gate from
Morpeth Road (B6344)
[81: NU073022]

Soil Acid, light soil

Terrain Steep hillside

Altitude 152m/499ft

Area 16 hectares/40 acres

Gardeners 4 full-time, 1 seasonal

♿ Partially accessible

🦮 Guide dogs allowed

Events Guided walks, children's
activity leaflets

Other gardens in the area
Wallington
Belsay Hall (not NT)

Cragside has one of Britain's finest high-Victorian gardens that is open to visitors. The rock garden is amongst the largest in Europe and is probably the last surviving example of its type. A fine collection of conifers, mainly from North America, is to be found in the pinetum, below Cragside House, and across the valley lie the three terraces of the formal garden. On the middle terrace is the orchard house, the only remaining glasshouse in the gardens, which was built for the culture of early fruit. Nearby are the stone-framed carpet beds, planted for the summer season and on the terrace just below is the dahlia walk.

Restoration is still in progress on the bottom, or Italian, terrace, which contains a fine loggia and an imposing quatrefoil pool. Finally, the valley garden itself is yet to be developed, but provides a wonderful setting for a gentle stroll.

The orchard house, and display of potted plants, 19th-century style
(NTPL/Rupert Truman)

Croome Park

Capability Brown's first complete design comprising outer shelter belts, parkland, a mile-long artificial river, a series of shrubberies winding through the park, a collection of garden buildings by Brown, Robert Adam and James Wyatt, and an orchard, all surrounding a mansion designed by Brown (not NT). Good woodland birds all year, and butterflies in July and August, including Marbled White. The parkland is currently undergoing conversion from arable to grassland.

Apr	violets, primroses
May	bluebells, Manna Ash
Jun	
Jul	butterflies, including Marbled White
Aug	
Sep	
Oct	
Win	closed

NT Estate Office, The Builders' Yard, High Green, Severn Stoke, Worcestershire WR8 9JS
Tel 01905 371006
Fax 01905 371090
Email croomepark@ntrust.org.uk

Location (6:D9) 8ml S of Worcester and E of A38 and M5, 6ml W of Pershore, and A44 [150: SO887453]

Soil Clayey, some over marl, some over limey shales

Terrain Shallow valley with bordering scarp slope facing west on eastern boundary

Altitude 17-33m/56-108ft

Area 270 hectares/667 acres

Gardeners 1 full-time

Great gardeners Capability Brown, John Graefer

 Partially accessible

Guide dogs allowed

Plant sales Plant fair in May

Other gardens in the area
Hanbury Hall
Great Witley (not NT)
Little Malvern Priory (not NT)
Pershore College (not NT)
Spetchley Park (not NT)

Sabrina, nymph of the River Severn, reclining in the 18th-century grotto. (NTPL/Vera Collingwood)

Dudmaston

Apr	daffodils
May	azaleas, rhododendrons, magnolias
Jun	cistus
Jul	roses, agapanthus, fuchsias
Aug	campanulas, eucryphias
Sep	late perennials
Oct	autumn colour
Win	closed

Informal, with sweeping lawns overlooking pools, this is a spring-flowering garden with a superb collection of azaleas, rhododendrons and magnolias. Acers give good autumn colour. There is a handsome rockery, rose border, bog garden and a recently replanted herbaceous border. An interesting collection of contemporary sculpture. Lakeside and Dingle Walk, lovely views looking out to Clee Hills.

Quatt, nr Bridgnorth, Shropshire
WV15 6QN
Tel 01746 780866
Fax 01746 780744
Email dudmaston@ntrust.org.uk

Location (6:C7) 4ml SE of
Bridgnorth on A442
[138: SO746887]

Soil Acid to neutral, loamy/sandy

Terrain Undulating

Altitude 75m/246ft

Area 3.2 hectares/8 acres

Gardeners 2 full-time

Great gardeners Walter 'Planter' Wood

 Fully accessible

 Scented plants, guide dogs allowed

Plant sales Herbs

Other gardens in the area
Benthall Hall
Berrington Hall
Wightwick Manor
Hodnet (not NT)

Bronze boxing hares, by Barry Flanagan (NTPL/John Hammond)

Dunham Massey

Not only one of the plantsman's gardens of north-west England, but also of considerable historic interest. The moat and mount are early features, later becoming part of a wider formal layout in the 19th-century French style. The exquisite orangery survives and, closer to the house, the Edwardian parterre. Elsewhere, the moist acid conditions and varied site are home to natural plantings of shade- and moisture-loving plants. Highlights include Himalayan blue poppies in spring, giant Chinese lilies and late-flowering azaleas in early summer, followed by mixed borders. Extensive collection of hydrangeas. Paths around spacious lawns and through woodland are wheelchair-friendly.

Apr	spring woodland planting
May	rhododendrons
Jun	Himalayan blue poppies
Jul	giant Chinese lilies, mixed borders
Aug	hydrangeas
Sep	hydrangeas
Oct	pampas grasses
Win	closed

Altrincham, Greater Manchester
WA14 4SJ
Tel 0161 941 1025
Fax 0161 929 7508
Email
dunhammassey@ntrust.org.uk

Location (7:K7) 3ml SW of Altrincham off A56; exit 19 off M6; exit 7 off M56
[109: SJ735874]

Soil Acid sand

Terrain Level

Altitude 25m/82ft

Area 10 hectares/25 acres

Gardeners 5 full-time

Fully accessible

Guide dogs allowed

Plant sales Plantsman's Day held Sunday after 1st May BH

Other gardens in the area
Hare Hill
Tatton Park
Arley Hall (not NT)
Ness Botanical Gardens (not NT)

White *Eremurus himilaicus* in the east border
(NTPL/Neil Campbell-Sharp)

Dunster Castle

Apr	camellias
May	bluebells, primroses, violets, cherry blossom, magnolias
Jun	citrus collection, olive collection, roses
Jul	handkerchief tree, tender plants
Aug	hydrangeas
Sep	arbutus collection
Oct	autumn colour
Win	snowdrops, daffodils

Dunster, nr Minehead, Somerset
TA24 6SL
Tel 01643 821314
Fax 01643 823000
Email dunstercastle@ntrust.org.uk

Location (1:G5) In Dunster, 3ml
SE of Minehead. NT car park
approached direct from A39
[181: ST995439]

Soil Acid, light soil

Terrain Very steep

Altitude 15m/49ft

Area 6.8 hectares/17 acres

Gardeners 3 full-time

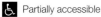 Partially accessible

 Scented plants, guide dogs
allowed

Events Walks and talks with
head gardener, bat walks, open-
air theatre, Easter egg hunt

Other gardens in the area
Knightshayes Court
Cannington College Gardens (not
NT)
Combe Sydenham (not NT)
Hestercombe Gardens (not NT)

A steep, wooded garden surrounding Dunster Castle, first described by James Savage in 1830 when the tor was covered with evergreens, flowering trees and shrubs. The south-east slopes and terraces offer conditions suitable for tender sun-loving plants including palms and a 100-year-old lemon tree. Collections also include rhododendrons, camellias, magnolias, herbaceous and mixed borders. Winding paths give views over attractive parkland. The Mill Walk at the base of the tor was mostly planted by Mrs Alys Luttrell in the early 1920s and restored by the NT after receiving the property from Colonel Luttrell in 1976. Conservatory. National Collection of Arbutus.

Below: A corner of the conservatory (NTPL/Richard Allenby-Pratt)

Opposite: Neptune looking down on the east front of the house: the orangery is on the left (NTPL/Rupert Truman)

Dyrham Park

Little remains of the magnificent 17th-century water garden at Dyrham Park captured by Kip in his view of 1712. Now Dyrham's grounds are largely taken up by parkland planned by Charles Harcourt-Master in the 18th century, with fine trees including beeches, chestnuts and cedars. Fallow deer roam the parkland. The garden to the rear of the house includes flower and shrub beds and a large pond. The orangery has been restored to its early 18th-century layout. A lovely nut walk.

Apr	spring bulbs
May	spring bulbs, shrubs
Jun	summer flowering
Jul	summer flowering
Aug	later summer flowering
Sep	autumn colour
Oct	autumn colour
Win	March: spring bulbs

Dyrham, nr Chippenham,
Gloucestershire SN14 8ER
Tel/Fax 01179 372501
Email dyrhampark@ntrust.org.uk

Soil Silty loam

Terrain Gentle slopes

Altitude 136m/446ft

Area 3.24 hectares/8 acres

Gardeners 2 full-time, 1 part-time, 1 + 1 careership seasonal

Great gardeners George London, Humphry Repton

 Partially accessible

 Guide dogs allowed

Plant sales In shop

Events Guided walks, music weekend

Other gardens in the area
The Courts
Lacock Abbey
Prior Park
Westonbirt Arboretum (not NT)

Location (1:K4) 8ml N of Bath,12ml E of Bristol; approached from Bath–Stroud road (A46), 2ml S of Tormarton interchange with M4, exit 18 [172: ST743757]

East Riddlesden Hall

Apr	bulbs, spring flowers
May	prunus, roses, bulbs
Jun	clematis, philadelphus
Jul	honeysuckle, geranium
Aug	shrubs, cyclamen, agapanthus
Sep	sedum, euonymus
Oct	autumn colour
Win	closed

Bradford Road, Keighley,
Yorkshire BD20 5EL
Tel 01535 607075
Fax 01535 691462
Email
eastriddlesden@ntrust.org.uk

Location (8:B7) 1ml NE of
Keighley on S side of the
Bradford Road in Riddlesden,
close to Leeds & Liverpool Canal
[104: SE079421]

Soil Slightly acidic

Terrain Raised garden
overlooking Aire Valley

Altitude 100m/328ft

Area 1 hectare/2 acres

Gardeners 1 part-time

Great gardeners Graham Stuart
Thomas, William Robinson

 Partially accessible

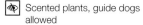 Scented plants, guide dogs
allowed

Events Plant fair, garden tours
by arrangement, children's
garden events

Other gardens in the area
Gawthorpe Hall
Golden Acre Park (not NT)
The Hollies (not NT)
Parceval Hall Gardens (not NT)
RHS Harlow Carr Botanical
   Gardens (not NT)

A 17th-century manor house set in attractive grounds with mature beech trees. The dramatic façade of the Starkie Wing provides a delightful backdrop to this small intimate garden designed by Graham Stuart Thomas. Planted with mixed herbaceous borders, trained fruit trees, lavender and herb border, based on Culpeper's *Herbal*. Formality is provided by a sunken rose garden planted with *Rosa* 'Marlena' and *Robinia pseudoacacia* 'Intermis'. The orchard garden, developed by the gardener and volunteers, is planted with old varieties of Yorkshire apple trees, wild flowers, bulbs and perennials, to provide a changing carpet of colour throughout the seasons.

Emmetts Garden

Laid out in the late 19th century in the informal style of the influential Victorian gardener William Robinson, this charming shrub garden is situated at the highest point in Kent. It contains many rare and exotic trees and shrubs from across the world in a natural landscape, underplanted with naturalised bulbs. An Italianate rose garden, created in 1910, and the rock garden, built in 1937, provide summer colour. Impressive displays of daffodils, bluebells, camellias and rhododendrons in spring.

Apr	daffodils
May	rhododendrons, bluebells
Jun	azaleas, rhododendrons
Jul	
Aug	eucryphia, hydrangeas
Sep	hydrangeas
Oct	autumn colour
Win	closed

Ide Hill, Sevenoaks, Kent
TN14 6AY
Tel 01732 750367 · 01732
868381 (Enquiries)
Fax 01732 750490
Email emmetts@ntrust.org.uk

Location (2:G6) 1½ml S of A25
on Sundridge to Ide Hill road,
1½ml N of Ide Hill off B2042,
leave M25 at exit 5, then 4ml
[188: TQ477524]

Soil Greensand over ragstone

Terrain Hillside

Altitude 240m/787ft

Area 7.5 hectares/19 acres

Gardeners 2 full-time

Partially accessible

Braille guide, scented
plants, guide dogs allowed

dogs allowed on leads

Other gardens in the area
Chartwell
Ightham Mote

Above: A carpet of bluebells
(NTPL/Jerry Harpur)

Opposite: The orchard garden
(NT/David Leighton)

Erddig

Apr	bulbs
May	spring bedding, blossom, bulbs
Jun	herbaceous borders
Jul	summer bedding, roses
Aug	summer bedding
Sep	fruit, autumn bedding
Oct	fruit, autumn colour
Win	closed

nr Wrexham, Wrexham LL13 0YT
Tel 01978 355314
Fax 01978 313333
Email erddig@ntrust.org.uk

Location (0:H3) 2ml S of
Wrexham, signposted A525
Whitchurch road, or A483/A5152
Oswestry road [117: SJ326482]

Soil Lime-free clays and loams

Terrain Level plateau falling away
to the west

One of the most significant surviving examples of an early 18th-century formal garden in Britain. The walled garden has been sympathetically restored following many years of neglect. Central path to the canal pond flanked by grand plats of lawn and apple orchards divided by pleached lime avenues. Original gravelled paths lead past espaliered fruit and climbing plants on garden walls. Later additions to the garden have also been restored, including the Victorian Parterre, Irish Yew Walk, Victorian Flower Garden and Rose Garden with spectacular clematis, herbaceous borders, Moss Walk shrubbery, extensive herb border and newly-restored Victorian glasshouses. National Collection of Ivy.

Altitude 60m/197ft

Area 5.2 hectares/13 acres

Gardeners 4 full-time

 Partially accessible

 Braille guide, scented
plants, guide dogs allowed

Plant sales A selection of herbs,
shrubs and climbers

Events Guided walks, apple
festival, theatre, children's events

Other gardens in the area
Chirk Castle
Powis Castle

Clematis montana
scrambling over the
walls (NTPL/Stephen
Robson)

Farnborough Hall

Untouched 18th-century garden elysium designed by William Holbech c.1745 with advice from Sanderson Miller. Series of pools adapted from a string of stewponds. Serpentine terraced walk ascends from house, punctuated by an Ionic temple and oval pavilion and terminating with an obelisk, providing fine views. Rose garden, daffodils, flowers in urns, cascade and superb Cedar of Lebanon.

Apr	daffodils
May	spring bulbs
Jun	wistaria, papavers
Jul	roses
Aug	herbaceous shrubs, pelargoniums, lilies
Sep	autumn foliage
Oct	closed
Win	closed

Banbury, Warwickshire
OX17 1DU
Tel 01295 690002
Email
farnboroughhall@ntrust.org.uk

Location (6:F8) 6ml N of
Banbury, ½ml W of A423
[151: SP430490]

Soil Loam over clay

Terrain Sheltered site

Altitude 150m/492ft

Area 3.2 hectares/8 acres

Gardeners 1 full-time

Partially accessible

Guide dogs allowed

Other gardens in the area
Canons Ashby
Charlecote Park
Hidcote Manor
Stowe Landscape Gardens
Upton House
Batsford (not NT)
Kiftsgate Court (not NT)

The oval pavilion, built in the mid-18th century by William Holbech
(NTPL/Matthew Antrobus)

63

Felbrigg Hall

Apr	blossom, bluebells
May	blossom, azaleas, rhododendrons, potagers
Jun	roses, borders
Jul	borders
Aug	borders
Sep	borders, fruit
Oct	autumn crocus, fruit
Win	closed

Felbrigg, Norwich, NR11 8PR
Tel 01263 837444
Fax 01263 837032
Email felbrigg@ntrust.org.uk

Location (4:K2) Nr Felbrigg village, 2ml SW of Cromer; entrance off B1436, signposted from A148 and A140 [133: TG193394]

Soil Lime-free

Terrain Level

Altitude 61m/200ft

Area 2.6 hectares/6 acres

Gardeners 2 full-time

Fully accessible

Braille guide, scented plants, guide dogs allowed

Other gardens in the area
Blickling Hall
Sheringham Park

Felbrigg is a garden of two halves. The West Garden, with its lovely 18th-century orangery, is largely an example of a typical Victorian pleasure ground, focusing upon the play between light and shade. Open formal lawns drift into dense and dark shrubbery. This area contains many fine specimen trees of transatlantic origin, including Red Oaks, Western Red Cedars and Giant Redwoods. To the east of the Hall lies the walled garden with its working 18th-century dovecote. Here are double borders of mixed shrubs, including roses, fuchsias and hydrangeas, herbaceous borders, a ribbon border and a hot border. Between these two main areas is the Garden Meadow, with a splendid sweet chestnut tree.

The kitchen garden produces vegetables and cut flowers, and there is an orchard with many varieties of cherries, apples, pears and plums – these are also trained against the walls along with figs, apricots and peaches. Felbrigg holds the National Collection of Colchicums.

Right: Detail of an espaliered peach in the walled garden (NTPL/Rob Matheson)

Opposite: Glass bell jars, herbs and vegetables in the kitchen garden (NTPL/Stephen Robson)

Fenton House

Delightful walled and terraced garden of 17th-century Hampstead house. Seasonal herbaceous borders edged with box. Some borders feature scented herbs and perennials such as lavender, rosemary and dianthus. A sunken rose garden (replanted 2000-2001) provides a colourful display in summer. Orchard with mature fruit trees underplanted with spring bulbs. Established espaliered trees surround the kitchen garden which contains a wide selection of vegetables. Next to the glasshouse is a new herb border, with mainly culinary herbs.

Apr	orchard, spring border
May	orchard spring border
Jun	roses
Jul	roses, herbaceous, vegetables
Aug	herbaceous, vegetables
Sep	herbaceous, vegetables, fruit
Oct	fruit
Win	orchard, spring border

Windmill Hill, Hampstead,
London NW3 6RT
Tel/Fax 020 7435 3471
Email fentonhouse@ntrust.org.uk

Location (3:G4) Visitors'
entrance on W side of
Hampstead Grove
[176:TQ262860]

Soil Sandy loam with pockets of clay

Terrain Mainly flat but terraced

Altitude 100m/328ft

Area 0.6 hectares/1 acre

Gardeners 1 full-time

 Partially accessible

Braille guide, scented plants, guide dogs allowed

Events NGS Open Evening, Paint the Garden Day, Easter Egg Hunt, Apple Day

Other gardens in the area
Kenwood (not NT)

Florence Court

Apr	daffodils
May	rhododendrons, cherry blossom
Jun	roses
Jul	rose pergola
Aug	herbaceous borders
Sep	autumn colour
Oct	autumn colour
Win	snowdrops

Impressive estate of rolling landscape with many splendid mature trees and fine views. Created *c.*1789 by William King for the 1st Earl of Enniskillen. The pleasure ground to the south is rich in azaleas and rhododendrons. The original Irish or Florence Court yew (*Taxus baccata* 'Fastigiata') still grows on the estate. Many old features survive, including walled garden, summer-house, ice-house, eel-house and bridge, and are gradually being restored.

Enniskillen, Fermanagh
BT92 1DB
Tel 028 6634 8249
Fax 028 6634 8873
Email florencecourt@ntrust.org.uk

Location (1:E6) 8ml SW of Enniskillen via A4 Sligo road and A32 Swanlinbar road, 4ml from Marble Arch Caves [H175344]

Soil Acid

Terrain Hilly, rolling down to lakelands

Altitude 61m/200ft

Area 250 (estate) hectares/618 acres

Gardeners 1 full-time

 Fully accessible

 Scented plants, guide dogs allowed

dogs allowed on leads

Events Guided walks throughout season, Annual Country Fair in May

Gawthorpe Hall

In front of the Hall is a lawn surrounded by azaleas and mature deciduous trees. The Victorian North Parterre, designed by Sir Charles Barry, includes exotically-shaped foliage and golden privet. Small rose garden and pond. Woodland interspersed with rhododendrons and azaleas. Oaks, birches, ferns and bluebells and buttercup fields. Riverside walks. Stone and tiled urns designed by A. W. N. Pugin.

Apr	blossom, bluebells
May	azaleas, rhododendrons, ducklings
Jun	summer bedding
Jul	roses, bedding
Aug	bedding, trees, wildlife
Sep	bedding, trees, wildlife
Oct	autumn colour
Win	

Soil Acid

Terrain Flat lawned area, hilly woodland

Altitude 76m/249ft

Area 12 hectares/30 acres

Gardeners 1 part-time

Opposite: The rose garden (NT/Chris Hill)

Below: The Victorian North Parterre (NTPL/Matthew Antrobus)

Great gardeners Sir Charles Barry

 Partially accessible

 Scented plants, guide dogs allowed

dogs allowed on leads

Plant sales Three a year

Events Guided walks, nature trails, outdoor theatre, fairs

Other gardens in the area
East Riddlesden Hall
Rufford Old Hall

Padiham, nr Burnley, Lancashire BB12 8UA
Tel 01282 771004
Fax 01282 770178
Email
gawthorpehall@ntrust.org.uk

Location (7:K5) On E outskirts of Padiham; ¾ml drive to house on N of A671; M65 jct 8 towards Clitheroe, then signposted from second traffic light junction [103: SD806340]

Glendurgan

Apr	magnolias, rhododendrons
May	rhododendrons, bluebells
Jun	aquilegia
Jul	Tulip tree
Aug	eucryphias
Sep	hydrangeas
Oct	autumn colour
Win	camellias, azaleas, magnolias, rhododendrons,

Mawnan Smith, nr Falmouth,
Cornwall TR11 5JZ
Tel 01326 250906 (opening
hours only) or 01872 862090
Fax 01872 865808
Email glendurgan@ntrust.org.uk

Location (1:C9) 4ml SW of
Falmouth, ½ml SW of Mawnan
Smith, on road to Helford
Passage [204: SW772277]

Soil Lime-free heavy soil

Terrain Steep, divided over 3
valleys

Altitude 10-70m/33-230ft

Area 13 hectares/32 acres

Gardeners 3 full-time

Not suitable for wheelchairs

Events Occasional guided walks

Other gardens in the area
Trelissick
Trengwainton
Bosvigo (not NT)
Carwinion (not NT)
Penjerrick (not NT)
Probus Demonstration Garden
    (not NT)
Trebah (not NT)
Trevarno (not NT)
Trewithen (not NT)

A garden of great beauty, created in the 1820s, running down to the tiny village of Durgan and its beach. Glendurgan is a woodland garden over three valleys, converging on the Helford River. Alfred Fox originally planted the garden in the 1820s and '30s, many of the plants having been brought to the country by sea captains who sailed on the Fox ships out of Falmouth. There are many fine trees and rare and exotic plants with outstanding magnolias and camellias. Late in the season glorious displays of wild flowers carpet the valley slopes. Special features include the cherry laurel maze dating from 1833, bamboo bridge, Giant's Stride, and the Holy Bank containing plants with biblical connections.

The cherry laurel maze
(NTPL/Stephen Robson)

Opposite: The fountain in the
Victorian fernery
(NTPL/Stephen Robson)

Greenway

The garden lies on the east bank of the River Dart, the slopes facing south west. A wooded valley with open areas in which many half-hardy trees and shrubs thrive. Managed in as natural a state as possible, Greenway boasts a superb plant collection with great rarities from all over the world, but mainly from the southern hemisphere. The garden has a mysterious, wild character with stunning native flora.

Note: The Trust is required to restrict the number of vehicles admitted to Greenway, and there is no parking space on the narrow country lanes leading to the property. All visitors, including National Trust members, will need to book parking space (tel. 01803 842382) before arriving at the property.

Apr	acacias, magnolias, viburnums, eucalyptus
May	davidias, embothriums, paulownias, enkianthus, drimys
Jun	rehderodendron, styrax
Jul	liriodendron, magnolias
Aug	catalpa, magnolias
Sep	eucryphias, clerodendrons
Oct	autumn colour
Win	camellias, magnolias

Greenway Road, Galmpton, nr
Churston Ferrers, Devon
TQ5 0ES
Tel 01803 842382
Fax 01803 661900
Email greenway@ntrust.org.uk

Soil pH5.5-7, very open shale

Terrain Steep valley

Altitude 0-60m/0-197ft

Area 15 hectares/37 acres

Gardeners 3 full-time

Great gardeners Williams family

 Partially accessible

 Braille guide, scented plants, guide dogs allowed

Events Guided walks by appointment

Other gardens in the area
Coleton Fishacre
Compton Castle
Overbecks
Plant World (not NT)

Location (1:G8) All visitors wishing to arrive by car must pre-book their parking space on 01803 842382. Unbooked cars will be turned away. Midi coaches (up to 25 seats) only can be accepted, again pre-booking essential. For details of green transport routes to Greenway, please phone 01803 842382.

Greys Court

Apr	spring bulbs
May	wistaria, peonies
Jun	roses, peonies, lilies
Jul	herbaceous, borders
Aug	herbaceous, borders
Sep	hydrangeas
Oct	closed
Win	closed

Rotherfield Greys, Henley-on-Thames, Oxfordshire RG9 4PG
Tel 01491 628529
Email greyscourt@ntrust.org.uk

Location (2:D5) W of Henley-on-Thames. From Nettlebed mini-roundabout on A4130 take the B481 and the property is signed to the left after about 3 miles. There is also a direct (unsigned) route from Henley-on-Thames town centre if you follow the signs to Peppard and Greys for about 3 miles [175: SU725834]

Soil Clay with flint

Terrain Mainly level

Altitude 75m/246ft

Area 1.2 hectares/3 acres

Gardeners 2 full-time, 1 seasonal

Partially accessible

Scented plants, guide dogs allowed

Events Please contact the property for details

Other gardens in the area
Cliveden
Hughenden Manor
West Wycombe Park
Stonor Park (not NT)

The brick and flint Tudor house is set in the courtyard of a medieval manor. The remains of the 14th-century fortifications form a series of walled gardens: a white garden features magnolias, lilies and peonies; the rose garden, planted with old-fashioned roses, leads to a circular walled garden enclosing ancient wistarias. The wall of the medieval tithe barn partly encloses a walk of Japanese cherry trees. The walled kitchen garden, planted with espaliered fruit and vegetables, supplies the house, staff and volunteers. Beyond the kitchen garden is the Archbishop's Maze, constructed from brick and grass and a statue of St Fiacre, patron saint of gardeners, stands at the bottom of an avenue of Morello cherry trees flanked by *Rosa mundi*.

Japanese cherries in blossom within the walls of the tithe barn (NTPL/Vera Collingwood)

Gunby Hall

Brick-walled 17th-century gardens with contemporary dovecote. Arched pergolas of fruit trees; herbaceous and cutting borders; roses and a herb garden in generous profusion. The kitchen garden contains an old-fashioned mixture of vegetables, fruit and flowers. Lawns to the east of the house extend to a wild garden and shrubbery. Much planting took place early in the 19th century by Peregrine Massingberd and again in the early 20th century by Margaret Massingberd. Formal planting of yews as bowling alleys to the west of the house date from c.1900. Other features include a large Cedar of Lebanon, ghost walk pond and wild flower walk.

Apr	large bulb collection
May	blossom, herbaceous borders
Jun	roses, herbaceous borders
Jul	roses, herbaceous borders
Aug	cut flower borders, roses, herbs, herbaceous borders
Sep	late borders, orchards
Oct	closed
Win	closed

Gunby, nr Spilsby, Lincolnshire PE23 5SS
Tel 0870 458 4000

Location (5:F5) 2½ml NW of Burgh le Marsh, 7ml W of Skegness on S side of A158 (access off roundabout) [122: TF467668]

Domed garden seat set in the herbaceous borders (NTPL/Rupert Truman)

Soil Alkaline, varies from clay to silt

Terrain Flat

Altitude 30m/98ft

Area 2.8 hectares/7 acres

Gardeners 2 full-time, 3 volunteers seasonal

Partially accessible

Scented plants, guide dogs allowed

Plant sales On Open Days

Events NGS days, Summer Fête, Autumn Fair

Other gardens in the area
Belton House
Burghley House (not NT)

71

Ham House

Apr	fritillaries and spring flowers
May	saxifrage, wistaria
Jun	cut flowers
Jul	hibiscus, pomegranates
Aug	lavender, hibiscus, pomegranates
Sep	lavender
Oct	field maples
Win	geometric and formal structure

Ham, Richmond, London
(Richmond-upon-Thames)
TW10 7RS
Tel 020 8940 1950
Fax 020 8332 6903
Email hamhouse@ntrust.org.uk

Location (3:F5) On S bank of
Thames, W of A307, between
Richmond and Kingston; Ham
Gate exit of Richmond Park,
readily accessible from M3, M4
and M25 [176: TQ172732]

Soil Acidic sandy loam

Terrain Flat, flood plain on
S bank of Thames

Altitude 15m/49ft

Area 44 hectares/109 acres

Gardeners 4 full-time

 Partially accessible

Guide dogs allowed

Plant sales In shop area

Events Plant fair, guided tours,
garden workshops, family events

Other gardens in the area
Chelsea Physic Garden (not NT)
Kew Gardens (not NT)
Hampton Court (not NT)
Palm Centre, Ham Street, Ham
(not NT)
RHS Wisley (not NT)
Syon Park (not NT)

Seventeenth-century formality predominates in this comprehensively restored garden, once the home of the beautiful and notorious Civil War spy, Elizabeth, Countess of Dysart. The strongly architectural nature of the wilderness, gravel terraces and parterres of cotton lavender, together with copies of the 17th-century furniture and summer-houses, add to the charm and interest of this all-year-round riverside garden. The borders are planted in repeated structural patterns in 17th-century style based on contemporary inventories.

The completion of a conservation plan has highlighted two areas for restoration as a priority. A kitchen garden development, standing in front of the orangery, will show the difference between those of the 17th century and the more commonly surviving Victorian examples. The wilderness is a rare and important survival and its future development will be based on a painting of 1675 by Dankerts of the south elevation of the house and gardens.

Cotton lavender and box cones in the East Garden.
(NTPL/Stephen Robson)

Hanbury Hall

Recreated early 18th-century formal garden designed by George London, including a sunken parterre, fruit garden, wilderness and grove featuring summer-houses, an obelisk, pool and pavilions. There is an orangery complete with citrus plants and other tender greens that are sited round the garden from June to early September. Behind the orangery is a working mushroom house dated from 1860. At the far end of the garden is a mid-18th-century ice-house which could hold 24 tons of ice. The bowling green is under reconstruction and due to open in 2002.

Apr	bulbs
May	bulbs
Jun	bowling green
Jul	parterre
Aug	pomegranate
Sep	apples
Oct	apples
Win	closed

The sunken parterre, planted to the designs of George London (NTPL/Nick Meers)

Droitwich, Worcestershire
WR9 7EA
Tel 01527 821214
Fax 01527 821251
Email hanburyhall@ntrust.org.uk

Location (6:D8) 4½ml E of Droitwich, 1ml N of B4090, 6ml S of Bromsgrove, 1½ml W of B4091 [150: SO943637]

Soil Neutral clay

Terrain Flat

Altitude 66m/217ft

Area 8 hectares/20 acres

Gardeners 3 full-time

Great gardeners George London

[♿] Partially accessible

[🦮] Guide dogs allowed

Plant sales Spring plant fair

Other gardens in the area
Baddesley Clinton
Coughton Court
Hidcote Manor
Packwood House
Bredon Springs (not NT)
The Priory (not NT)
Spetchley Park (not NT)

Hardwick Hall

Apr	orchard blossom, daffodils
May	
Jun	herb garden, roses
Jul	herb garden, roses
Aug	herbaceous borders
Sep	herbaceous borders
Oct	autumn colour
Win	closed

Doe Lea, Chesterfield,
Derbyshire S44 5QJ
Tel 01246 850430
Fax 01246 854200
Email hardwickhall@ntrust.org.uk

Location (5:C5) Note: A one-
way traffic system operates in
the Park; access only via
Stainsby Mill entrance (leave M1,
exit 29, follow brown signs), exit
only via Hardwick Inn. Park gates
shut 6 in summer, 5.30 in winter.
6½ml W of Mansfield, 9½ml SE of
Chesterfield; approach from M1
(exit 29) via A6175
[120: SK463638]

Soil Alkaline

Terrain Level

Altitude 200m/656ft

Area 3.6 hectares/9 acres

Gardeners 4 + 2 trainees full-time

 Partially accessible

Scented plants, guide dogs
allowed

Events Paint the Garden, guided
tours

Other gardens in the area
Clumber Park
Kedleston Hall
Chatsworth (not NT)
Haddon Hall (not NT)
Newstead Abbey (not NT)
Renishaw Hall (not NT)

Only walls and gazebos remain of Bess of Hardwick's late 16th-century garden. The present layout of the South Garden dates from the 1870s: grass alleys flanked by yew and hornbeam hedges planted by Lady Louisa Egerton, daughter of the 7th Duke of Devonshire, divide the garden into quadrants. Orchards, lawns, nuttery and herb garden (culinary, medicinal and dye-plants) occupy these four sections, conveying the spirit of an Elizabethan garden. West Courtyard laid out c.1920 by Blanche, daughter of the 9th Duke. Her mother, the Duchess Evelyn sank the pond in the East Court to provide water for fire-fighting. She also planted the double avenue called 'The Wineglass' that closes the eastern vista. Lead statues in yew alcoves, holly domes to the western entrance to the herb garden, grass walks, mulberry avenue.

Garden history exhibition in the south-east gazebo shows the garden's development over 400 years.

Detail of *Allium Porrum* (wild leek) in the herb garden
(NTPL/Stephen Robson)

Hardy's Cottage

Thomas Hardy, novelist and poet, was born in the cottage on 2 June 1840, and it was here he wrote *Far from the Madding Crowd*. A colourful cottage garden set out with beds, borders and small lawns around which gravel paths wind. Beyond this is an orchard with apples and medlar. The garden is surrounded by broad-leaved woodland and part of the original heath, which is being gradually restored. In 2001 the National Trust began a programme of low-key restoration of the outbuildings and other features within the grounds.

Apr	daffodils, primroses
May	aquilegia, tulips
Jun	lupins, irises
Jul	buddleia, evening primroses
Aug	golden rod
Sep	Michaelmas daisies, nasturtiums
Oct	
Win	closed

Higher Bockhampton, nr Dorchester, Dorset DT2 8QJ
Tel 01305 262366

Soil Acid

Terrain Undulating

Altitude approx 100m/328ft

Area 0.8 hectares/2 acres

Gardeners 3 part-time

 Partially accessible

Scented plants, guide dogs allowed

Other gardens in the area
Kingston Lacy

Location (1:K7) 3ml NE of Dorchester, ½ml S of A35
[194: SY728925]

The cottage garden (NTPL/Eric Crichton)

Hare Hill

Apr	
May	rhododendrons, spring flowers
Jun	
Jul	
Aug	
Sep	
Oct	autumn colour
Win	closed

Over Alderley, Macclesfield,
Cheshire SK10 4QB
Tel 0870 458 4000

Location (7:L8) Between
Alderley Edge and Prestbury,
turn off north at B5087 at
Greyhound Road
[118: SJ875765]

Soil Reddish till with surface
deposits of boulder clay

Terrain Dips and hollows

Altitude 120-150m/394-492ft

Area 4 hectares/10 acres

Gardeners 1 full-time, 1 part-time

Great gardeners James Russell

♿ Partially accessible

♿ Braille guide, scented
plants, guide dogs allowed

Other gardens in the area
The Apprentice House Garden,
   Quarry Bank Mill
Dunham Massey
Lyme Park
Tatton Park

A woodland garden with excellent planting including azaleas, rhododendrons, a fine collection of hollies, hostas and a rockery. It was laid out *c.*1820 when Hare Hill was built, although the main developments in the walled garden took place in the latter part of the 19th century. The delightful walled garden contains a pergola and wire sculptures. The area around the walled garden, although planted with some exotic species in the 19th century, was mainly developed in the last century by Colonel Charles Brocklehurst with advice from James Russell. The surrounding parkland has attractive walks, including a link path to Alderley Edge (2ml).

Wistaria growing over the
pergola in the walled garden
(NTPL/Geoff Morgan)

Hatchlands Park

The small, formal box garden, designed by the eminent local designer Gertrude Jekyll in 1913-14, has been restored to reflect its original glory. Miniature hedging surrounds flower-beds filled with old-fashioned roses, irises, peonies and other popular Edwardian plants. A statue of Paris looks from the edge of the garden away from the classical stone temple towards the 18th-century house. A giant London plane is underplanted with spring bulbs, while wild flowers provide a wash of colour in the surrounding grassland. Hatchlands also contains 160ha (395 acres) of woodland and Repton parkland, and there are three way-marked family trails and picnic tables. The woods are full of bluebells in May and the Sheepwash Pond provides a haven for waterfowl.

Apr	
May	Jekyll garden, bluebells
Jun	Jekyll garden
Jul	Jekyll garden
Aug	Jekyll garden
Sep	
Oct	autumn colour
Win	closed

East Clandon, Guildford, Surrey
GU4 7RT
Tel 01483 222482
Fax 01483 223176
Email hatchlands@ntrust.org.uk

Location (2:F6) E of East Clandon, N of A246 Guildford–Leatherhead road [187: TQ063516]

Soil Heavy, acid

Terrain Level

Altitude 90m/295ft

Area 430 hectares/1063 acres

Gardeners 2 full-time

Great gardeners Gertrude Jekyll, Humphry Repton

 Fully accessible

 Braille guide, scented plants, guide dogs allowed

Events Wildlife Trail

Other gardens in the area
Clandon Park
Claremont
Ham House
Winkworth Arboretum
Wisley RHS Garden (not NT)

Stone urn in a corner of the Jekyll garden (NTPL/Ian Shaw)

Hidcote Manor

Apr	spring bulbs
May	tulips
Jun	roses, herbaceous borders
Jul	herbaceous borders
Aug	summer perennials
Sep	herbaceous borders
Oct	autumn colour
Win	closed

Hidcote Bartrim, nr Chipping
Campden, Gloucestershire
GL55 6LR
Tel 01386 438333
Fax 01386 438817
Email hidcote@ntrust.org.uk

Location (1:M1) 4ml NE of
Chipping Campden, 1ml E of
B4632 (originally A46), off
B4081.

Coaches are not permitted
through Chipping Campden High
Street. Contact Campden TIC for
further information
[151: SP176429]

Hill-top Arts & Crafts garden created from 1907
onwards by Lawrence Johnston, a superb plantsman
and horticulturist. Archetype of garden with room-like
enclosures, each with a separate theme, set within an
architectural layout. Each garden has a unique
character and colour scheme and is separated from its
neighbours by walls and hedges of different species.
Many rare shrubs and trees, outstanding herbaceous
borders, old roses and unusual plant varieties, some of
which, such as *Verbena* 'Lawrence Johnston' and
Hypericum 'Hidcote', bearing the Johnston or Hidcote
names, were developed here.

Soil Alkaline

Terrain Level site

Altitude 182m/597ft

Area 4 hectares/10 acres

Gardeners 7 full-time

Great gardeners Lawrence
Johnston

 Partially accessible

Scented plants, guide dogs
allowed, audio guide

Plant sales Plant centre
adjacent to car park

Other gardens in the area
Snowshill Manor
Batsford (not NT)
Kiftsgate Court (not NT)
Sezincote (not NT)

The Red Borders
(NTPL/Andrew Lawson)

Hill Top

This charming, traditional cottage garden, at the former home of Beatrix Potter, is tightly packed with a miscellany of flowers, fruit and vegetables. With the help of illlustrations in her 'little books', and using contemporary photographs, the garden has been restored to look much as it did in the author's day, with many original garden features remaining.

Apr	spring bulbs
May	wistaria
Jun	foxgloves
Jul	soft fruit
Aug	roses, eucryphia
Sep	dahlias
Oct	autumn colour
Win	closed

Near Sawrey, Ambleside, Cumbria LA22 0LF
Tel 015394 36269
Fax 015394 36118
Email hilltop@ntrust.org.uk

Location (7:C6) 2ml S of Hawkshead, in hamlet of Near Sawrey, behind the Tower Bank Arms [96/97: SD370955]

Soil Acid, stony

Terrain Gently sloping

Altitude 110m/361ft

Area 0.2 hectares/0.5 acres

Gardeners 1 part-time

♿ Partially accessible

Scented plants, guide dogs allowed

Other gardens in the area
Sizergh Castle
Stagshaw
Brockhole (not NT)
Holehird (not NT)

The cottage garden
(Stephen Robson)

Hinton Ampner

Apr	spring bulbs, viburnums, bedding
May	spring bulbs, viburnums, bedding
Jun	roses, shrubs
Jul	shrubs, tender summer planting, argyranthemums, osteospermums
Aug	shrubs, tender summer planting, salvias
Sep	late season plants, salvias, hibiscus, abelias
Oct	closed
Win	closed

One of the great gardens of the 20th century. A masterpiece of design by Ralph Dutton, 8th and last Lord Sherborne, uniting a formal layout of immaculate hedges and topiary with varied and informal plantings in mainly pastel shades. A garden of considerable interest to the plant enthusiast, with scented plants, fine lawns and terraces and magnificent vistas over the park and rolling Hampshire countryside.

Bramdean, nr Alresford, Hampshire SO24 0LA
Tel 01962 771305
Fax 01962 793101
Email hintonampner@ntrust.org.uk

Location (2:D7) On A272, 1ml W of Bramdean village, 8ml E of Winchester, leave M3 at exit 9 and follow signs to Petersfield [185: SU597275]

P 🚻 🚶 ♿ 🍴

Soil Mainly alkaline over chalk

Terrain Fairly level

Altitude 122m/400ft

Area 5 hectares/12 acres

Gardeners 3 full-time

♿ Fully accessible

♿ Braille guide, scented plants, guide dogs allowed

Plant sales NT Spring Plant Fair

Other gardens in the area
Mottisfont Abbey
Uppark
The Vyne

The Yew Garden, with tulips and topiary (NTPL/Stephen Robson)

Hughenden Manor

The high-Victorian garden surrounding Disraeli's house was largely created by his wife, Mary Anne. Set in a delightfully wooded valley, the garden features a terrace decorated with vases to Mrs Disraeli's design. The unusual graft hybrid *Laburnocytisus* 'Adamii' grows in the garden. The 1880s formal bedding in the South Garden has been restored, and the orchard has been re-created, stocking 35 old varieties of apple and four varieties of pear.

Apr	wildflowers, bulbs
May	spring bedding
Jun	
Jul	summer bedding
Aug	summer bedding
Sep	summer bedding
Oct	
Win	closed Nov to end Feb

Formal bedding, 1880s style, in the South Garden (NTPL/Matthew Antrobus)

High Wycombe,
Buckinghamshire HP14 4LA
Tel 01494 755573
Fax 01494 474284
Email hughenden@ntrust.org.uk

Location (2:E4) 1½ml N of High Wycombe; on W side of the Great Missenden road (A4128) [165: SU866955]

Soil Limy soil

Terrain Level

Altitude 152m/499ft

Area 2 hectares/5 acres

Gardeners 1 full-time

 Partially accessible, Garden can be viewed by wheelchair users from terrace.

Plant sales Orchard produce for sale

Events Please contact the property for details

Other gardens in the area
Cliveden
West Wycombe Park

Ickworth

Apr	wild flowers
May	wallflowers
Jun	roses
Jul	herbaceous borders
Aug	geraniums
Sep	agapanthus
Oct	autumn colours
Win	spring bulbs, evergreen

Ickworth, The Rotunda,
Horringer, Bury St Edmunds,
Suffolk IP29 5QE
Tel 01284 735270
Fax 01284 735175
Email ickworth@ntrust.org.uk

Location (4:H6) In Horringer, 3ml
SW of Bury St Edmunds on W
side of A143 [155: TL8161]

Soil Heavy acid boulder clay

Terrain Level

Altitude 75m/246ft

Area 728 hectares/1799 acres

Gardeners 4 full-time, 1 part-
time, 2 seasonal

Great gardeners Capability
Brown

 Partially accessible

 Scented plants, guide dogs
allowed

Plant sales Plant Fair
(September)

Events Guided walks, Wood
Sale and Fair (April)

Other gardens in the area
Anglesey Abbey
Abbey Gardens, Bury St
   Edmunds (not NT)
Cambridge Botanic Gardens (not
   NT)
Kentwell Hall (not NT)

The grounds of Ickworth, designed to reflect the
Italianate, late 18th-century house commissioned by
the eccentric 4th Earl of Bristol, Frederick Augustus
Hervey, are heavily wooded with yews, evergreen oak
and box, and paths giving views of the central rotunda
from various points. The garden contains some
uncommon trees including a *Koelreuteria paniculata*
from north China. The Silver Garden, hidden among
the trees, boasts a collection of hexagonal stones from
the Giant's Causeway and Victorian stumpery.
A herbaceous border planted with boldly coloured
flowers fronts the north lawn. The orangery in the
west wing protects lemon trees and agapanthus in the
winter. The park surrounding the house contains
some of the best examples of ancient specimen trees
including oak, beech and hornbeam. Interesting
sculpture including Frink heads in Italian Garden, and
two spheres by Chris Drury along Albana Walk.
National Collection of *Buxus* (Box).

Agapanthus and pelargoniums on the steps of the rotunda
(NTPL/Neil Campbell-Sharp)

Ightham Mote

Lovely medieval moated manor house set in wooded valley. Cottage-style plantings around stable building, lawns and enclosed paved garden with lily pool. Cut flowers and vegetables planted with herbs along path edges. Long border with traditional flowers such as sweet williams, campanulas and pinks. Woodland with native and exotic trees and shrubs and interspersed with paths.

Apr	orchard, cottage borders
May	orchard, cottage borders
Jun	cottage borders, enclosed garden, vegetables, main border
Jul	cottage borders, enclosed garden, vegetables, main border
Aug	cottage borders, enclosed garden, vegetables, main border
Sep	cottage borders, enclosed garden, vegetables, main border
Oct	woodland walk
Win	closed

Soil Clay loam

Terrain Valley

Altitude 100m/328ft

Area 5.7 hectares/14 acres

Gardeners 3 full-time

 Partially accessible

Braille guide, scented plants, guide dogs allowed

Plant sales On NGS days

Events Garden tours

Other gardens in the area
Chartwell
Emmetts
Great Comp Garden (not NT)
Hever Castle (not NT)
Penshurst Place (not NT)

Ivy Hatch, Sevenoaks, Kent
TN15 0NT
Tel 01732 810378
Fax 01732 811029
Email
ighthammote@ntrust.org.uk

Location (2:H6) 6ml E of Sevenoaks, off A25, and 2½ml S of Ightham, off A227
[188: TQ584535]

View over the manor house to the north east garden
(NTPL/Andrew Butler)

Kedleston Hall

Apr	daffodils, primroses
May	rhododendrons, azaleas
Jun	rhododendrons, azaleas
Jul	roses, shrubs
Aug	roses
Sep	
Oct	autumn colour
Win	closed

Derby, Derbyshire DE22 5JH
Tel 01332 842191
Fax 01332 841972
Email kedlestonhall@ntrust.org.uk

Location (5:B6) 5ml NW of
Derby, entrance off Kedleston
Road and signposted from
roundabout where A38 crosses
A52 close to Markeaton Park
[SK312403]

Soil Acid

Terrain Level

Altitude 100m/328ft

Area 7 hectares/17 acres

Gardeners 2 full-time,
1 part-time

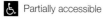 Partially accessible

Scented plants, guide dogs
allowed

Events Guided walks, rose
pruning workshop (March),
Garden fête

Other gardens in the area
Calke Abbey
Hardwick Hall
Sudbury Hall
Melbourne Hall (not NT)
Chatsworth (not NT)
Haddon Hall (not NT)
Ley Gardens (not NT)

Pleasure grounds and landscape park laid out by 1st
Lord Scarsdale with designs and buildings by Robert
Adam. A 3.5-mile walk swings round to the south of
the house, giving extensive views. The pleasure
grounds underwent some formalisation at the end of
the 19th century and between 1922 and 1924 when
Edwin Lutyens and Gertrude Jekyll advised. Present
planting re-establishes the 18th-century feel, with
contemporary garden buildings and monuments,
including the orangery (*c.*1800) and hexagonal
summerhouse, lying within the grounds, which are
planted with rhododendrons, shrubs and species trees.
In the park further buildings, including the bridge and
cascade, together with the fishing pavilion, are also the
work of Robert Adam. Fine specimens of *Fagus
sylvatica* 'Asplenifolia' and *Tilia platyphyllos*.

Killerton

The gardens were first laid out by Sir Thomas Acland, 7th Baronet, and his agent, John Veitch, when the house was rebuilt in 1777. Later, Veitch founded a famous firm of nurserymen which sent plant hunters (including the Lobb brothers and Ernest Wilson) all over the world to bring back new species, many of which found a home in Killerton garden. The garden was developed by successive generations of the Acland family. In the 1920s Sir Frances Acland, 14th Baronet, supported Captain Kingdon-Ward's plant-hunting expeditions to the Himalayas, which brought new rhododendron species to Killerton.

The herbaceous border and terrace were laid out in the early 20th century by William Robinson.

Apr	rhododendrons, camellias, magnolias
May	azeleas, wild flowers
Jun	herbaceous borders
Jul	herbaceous borders, roses
Aug	herbaceous borders
Sep	late herbaceous plants
Oct	autumn colour
Win	conifers, bark, bulbs

Broadclyst, Exeter, Devon
EX5 3LE
Tel 01392 811200
Fax 01392 883112
Email killerton@ntrust.org.uk

Location (1:G7) Off Exeter–Cullompton road (B3181, formerly A38); from M5 northbound, exit 30 via Pinhoe and Broadclyst; from M5 southbound, exit 28 [192: SX9700]

Soil Acid 4.5-5.5ph sandy loam

Terrain Steep, sloping to south

Altitude 50m/164ft

Area 9 hectares/22 acres

Gardeners 5 full-time

Great gardeners William Robinson, John Veitch

Partially accessible

Scented plants, guide dogs allowed

Plant sales Throughout year

Events Full programme – phone for details

Other gardens in the area
Castle Drogo
Knightshayes Court

Above: View down through the woodland garden to the Bear's Hut, a Victorian summer house (NTPL/Andrew Butler)

Opposite: The hexagonal summer-house in the pleasure grounds (NTPL/Mark Fiennes)

Kingston Lacy

Apr	flowering shrubs, anemone nemorosa
May	rhododendrons, camellias
Jun	roses
Jul	formal bedding
Aug	formal bedding, fernery
Sep	acers – autumn colour
Oct	acers – autumn colour
Win	snowdrops, pulmonarias

Wimborne Minster, Dorset
BH21 4EA
Tel 01202 883402 (Mon to Fri
9–5) & 01202 842913 (Sat & Sun
11–5)
Fax 01202 882402
Email kingstonlacy@ntrust.org.uk

Location (1:L7) On B3082
Blandford–Wimborne road, 1½ml
W of Wimborne [195: ST980019]

Soil Light soil mix, mainly chalky

Terrain Flat

Altitude 25m/82ft

Area 5.26 hectares/13 acres

Gardeners 4 full-time,
2 seasonal

 Fully accessible, (except
one gravel path)

 Guide dogs allowed

Plant sales Wide range of plants
for sale

Events Plant fairs, guided walks

Other gardens in the area
Compton Acres (not NT)
Cranborne Manor (not NT)
Knoll Gardens (not NT)
Stapehill Abbey (not NT)

The formal gardens and extensive parkland, with a prize-winning herd of Red Devon cattle, surround the 17th-century house designed by Sir Roger Pratt. The garden was overgrown when acquired by the NT in 1982 and has been extensively restored, particularly the Victorian fernery which contains 20 species of fern. Early snowdrops in spring are followed by daffodils and a fine collection of rhododendrons, azaleas, and bedding in the sunken garden and parterre. The Japanese Tea Garden is presently being restored. Children's play areas around the woodland walks. On the south lawn stands an ancient 33ft Egyptian obelisk, acquired on his travels by William Bankes in 1821. There are two National Collections: *Anemone Nemorosa* (Wood Anemone) and *Convallaria* (Lily of the Valley).

Formal parterre in front of the
house (NT)

Knightshayes Court

The original Victorian garden was designed by the celebrated landscaper Edward Kemp, but the present more extensive gardens owe much to the late Sir John and Lady Heathcoat Amory who gave Knightshayes to the NT in 1972. The Amorys together designed, planted and maintained growing collections of magnolia, rhododendron, unusual trees and shrubs, bulbs and herbaceous plants within their 'Garden in the Wood'. This is laid out beyond the formal lawns surrounded by battlemented yews, a topiary chase scene and a circular lily pool. Knightshayes is a collection of gardens linked together by design using plant texture and colour to provide interest from early springtime to the autumn.

The NT Plant Conservation Programme (not open to the public) propagates unusual plants and also accepts gifts of rare seed and young plants from around the world, which are grown on for distribution to other NT gardens. Knightshayes plant centre sells plants propagated from the garden.

Apr	crocus, anemone, magnolia, rhododendron, erythronium
May	narcissus, cornus, azelea, trillium, prunus, sorbus
Jun	herbaceous borders, roses, philadelphus, cistus, iris
Jul	herbaceous, viburnum, hoheria, eucryphia, peonies
Aug	crocosmia, lysimachia, anemone, dierama, clethra
Sep	hydrangea, agapanthus, colchicum, liriope, salvia
Oct	autumn colour and fruits
Win	closed

Bolham, Tiverton, Devon
EX16 7RQ
Tel 01884 254665
Fax 01884 243050
Email knightshayes@ntrust.org.uk

Location (1:G6) 2ml N of Tiverton; turn right off Tiverton–Bampton road (A396) at Bolham [181: SS960151]

Soil Fertile rich reddish acid to neutral overlaying sandstone shale

Terrain Undulating, mild SW prevailing winds

Altitude 136m/446ft

Area 20.2 hectares/50 acres

Gardeners 6 full-time

Partially accessible

Braille guide, scented plants, guide dogs allowed

Plant sales Plant centre

Other gardens in the area
Arlington Court
Dunster Castle
Killerton

A detail of the 'Garden in the Wood' (NTPL/Stephen Robson)

Lacock Abbey

Apr	spring flowers
May	trees
Jun	trees
Jul	trees
Aug	trees
Sep	trees
Oct	trees
Win	snowdrops, crocus, spring flowers

Lacock, nr Chippenham,
Wiltshire SN15 2LG
Tel Abbey Tel/Fax 01249 730227
Fax 01249 730501

Location (1:K4) 3ml S of
Chippenham, just E of A350;
signposted to car park
[173: ST919684]

Soil Neutral loam

Terrain Level

Altitude 30m/98ft

Area 3.6 hectares/9 acres

Gardeners 1 full-time, 1 seasonal

Great gardeners William Henry
Fox Talbot

 Fully accessible

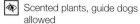 Scented plants, guide dogs
allowed

Plant sales Some

Events Guided walks in spring,
guided walks by arrangement,
plant fair, children's woodland trail

Other gardens in the area
The Courts
Bowood House (not NT)

Thirteenth-century abbey converted to a private house in the 16th century, surrounded by 19th-century woodland garden and 18th-century parkland thought to be the work of Capability Brown. The woodland contains many specimen trees, including black walnuts, swamp cypress, cedars, limes and a very fine Caucasian wing nut (*Pterocarya fraxinifolia*). The pioneer of photography, William Henry Fox Talbot, lived here during the 19th century and the woodland garden is the result of his botanical interests. So, too, is the newly-opened Botanic Garden, which contains collections of plants known to have interested him, including geraniums, campanulas, digitalis, eryngiums, euphorbias, and some tender Mediterranean plants. A clearing in the woodland contains a rose garden dedicated to Fox Talbot's mother, Lady Elizabeth.

Other features include an orchard, medieval stewpond with carp and 18th-century summer-house.

Impressive display of spring flowers including aconites, snakeshead fritillaries, anemones and winter crocus.

Spring bulbs with the abbey behind (NTPL/Ian Shaw)

Lanhydrock

Lanhydrock, overlooking the valley of the River Fowey, is a large 17th-century house rebuilt after a fire in 1881, with an apron of formal gardens, encircled by a horseshoe of hillsides, on which semi-formal trees and shrubs climb to merge with oak and beech woodland and shelter belts. The main part, or Higher Garden, contrasts with the formal area near the house and affords views out to the park including the double avenue, mainly beech, running for almost 1000 yards towards the river. Although the garden has its roots in the Victorian age, its collection is young with almost all the plants dating from the last 60 years. The Trust continues to build on the Victorian theme established by the Robartes family, magnolias and rhododendrons being particular features of the garden, together with herbaceous borders.

Apr	magnolias, camellias
May	rhododendrons
Jun	cornus
Jul	formal bedding, roses
Aug	bedding, roses
Sep	herbaceous border
Oct	herbaceous border
Win	spring bulbs

Bodmin, Cornwall PL30 5AD
Tel 01208 73320
Fax 01208 74084
Email lanhydrock@ntrust.org.uk

Location (1:D8) 2½ml SE of Bodmin, overlooking valley of River Fowey; follow signposts from either A30, A38 Bodmin–Liskeard or B3268 Bodmin–Lostwithiel roads [200: SX085636]

Soil Good medium loam pH4.5

Terrain Hillside

Altitude 100-130m/328-427ft

Area 12 hectares/30 acres

Gardeners 5 full-time

♿ Partially accessible

♿ Braille guide, scented plants, guide dogs allowed

Plant sales Daily in main car park, March–October

Other gardens in the area
Caerhays Castle (not NT)
The Eden Project (not NT)
The Lost Gardens of Heligan (not NT)
Pencarrow (not NT)
Pine Lodge Garden (not NT)
Tregrehan (not NT)

The parterre
(NTPL/Jerry Harpur)

89

Lavenham: The Guildhall of Corpus Christi

Apr	spring flowers
May	containers
Jun	roses
Jul	roses, dye plants
Aug	dye plants
Sep	dye plants
Oct	
Win	closed

Market Place, Lavenham,
Sudbury, Suffolk CO10 9QZ
Tel 01787 247646
Email
lavenhamguildhall@ntrust.org.uk

Location (4:H6) A1141 and
B1071 [155: TL917494]

Soil Loam, neutral pH

Terrain

Altitude valleym/ft

Area 0.4 hectares/1 acre

Gardeners 1 part-time

 Fully accessible

Scented plants, guide dogs
allowed

Other gardens in the area
Ickworth Park
Melford Hall

A small, tranquil walled garden with roses, lavender and borders. Plants grown here were used to dye the medieval cloth from which the village derived its wealth. Madder and safflower provided reds and pinks; weld and cardoon produced yellows and greens; woad, elecampane and viper's bugloss yielded blues. Teasels were used by the fullers to finish the cloth. Regular exhibitions and demonstrations are given by the local Guild of Weavers, Spinners and Dyers.

There is also a restored 19th-century lock-up and mortuary, as well as a Newsham fire engine, believed to be the oldest in East Anglia. A sundial has been commissioned for Her Majesty the Queen's Jubilee in 2002, with inscribed quotations from the coronations of Elizabeth I and Elizabeth II.

Right: The little walled garden planted with roses and dye plants (NTPL/Ray Hallett)

Opposite: The walled garden, looking towards the castle (NTPL/Joe Cornish)

Lindisfarne Castle

From 1902 the architect Edwin Lutyens turned the derelict Tudor castle into a holiday home for his friend and patron Edward Hudson. Another friend and patron, Gertrude Jekyll, designed the small walled garden set on a sheltered south-facing slope 500 yards from the castle, to be viewed from the bedroom windows. The garden was planned to provide cut flowers and salads for the house and a sheltered place to sit out. Jekyll's design included espaliered trees, vegetables and herbs with cottage garden plants. The NT is restoring this design.

Apr	
May	
Jun	
Jul	roses, herbaceous borders
Aug	herbaceous borders
Sep	
Oct	
Win	closed

Holy Island, Berwick-upon-Tweed, Northumberland
TD15 2SH
Tel 01289 389244
Fax 01289 389349

Soil Alkaline

Terrain Flat, exposed site

Altitude sea level

Area 1/8 acre hectares/44 acres

Gardeners 1 part-time

Great gardeners Gertrude Jekyll

 Not suitable for wheelchairs

 Scented plants, guide dogs allowed

🐕 dogs allowed on leads

Location (9:J4) On Holy Island, 6ml E of A1 across causeway [75: NU136417]

Little Moreton Hall

Apr	tulips, daffodils
May	tulips, herbs
Jun	tulips, vegetables, herbs, topiary
Jul	vegetables, herbs
Aug	vegetables, herbs
Sep	fruit
Oct	fruit
Win	closed

A garden bounded by a moat, with a 17th-century-style knot garden and yew tunnel. The herb garden and historic vegetable garden are planted with some of the earliest-known varieties grown in England: colewort, salsify, leaf beet, borecole, winter radish, haricot beans and marrowfat peas. Though no record of the original garden exists, layout and planting with period plants complement the timber-framed moated house.

Congleton, Cheshire CW12 4SD
Tel 01260 272018
Email
littlemoretonhall@ntrust.org.uk

Location (7:K9) 4ml SW of Congleton, on E side of A34 [118: SJ832589]

Soil Lime-free, sandy

Terrain Flat

Altitude 75m/246ft

Area 0.4 hectares/1 acre

Gardeners 1 full-time

Partially accessible

Braille guide, scented plants, guide dogs allowed

Plant sales At shop, May–Sept

Other gardens in the area
Biddulph Grange

The 17th-century-style knot garden (NTPL/Roy Twigge)

Llanerchaeron

A rare survivor of a Welsh gentry estate, bequeathed to the Trust by J.P. Ponsonby Lewes in 1989. The property is undergoing restoration and is open to visitors for a unique view of specialist work in progress. The house, designed by John Nash, sits in a designed landscape, possibly influenced by the Picturesque style, surrounded by pleasure grounds, 18th- and 19th-century walled gardens, home farm and parkland, as well as three vernacular cottages and a tenant farm. Detailed archaeological recording of extant structures in the walled gardens has greatly assisted in the restoration. Future work includes the restoration of the lake, as well as the glasshouses, cold frames and ponds. Ancient espaliers and apple trees give the walled garden its special historic character. The gardens are currently looked after by a group of volunteers led by a full-time gardener.

Apr	bulbs, daffodils
May	
Jun	roses
Jul	roses
Aug	apples, soft fruit
Sep	
Oct	
Win	garden closed, park open

nr Aberaeron, Ceredigion
SA48 8DG
Tel 01545 570200
Fax 01545 571759
Email
llanerchaeron@ntrust.org.uk

Location (0:E6) 2½ml east of Aberaeron off A482
[146: SN480 602]

Sunflower in one of the walled gardens (NTPL/Chris King)

Soil Clay

Terrain Aeron Valley, 2.5 miles from coast

Altitude 100m/328ft

Area 271 hectares/670 acres

Gardeners 1 full-time

 Fully accessible

Scented plants, guide dogs allowed

Plant sales Cut flowers, fruit and vegetables on sale every Thursday during visitor season.

Events Guided walks, plant fair, period costume day, daffodil days, Easter egg hunt, Flower, Herb and Vegetable Day

Other gardens in the area
National Botanic Garden of
    Wales (not NT)

Lyme Park

Apr	camellias, spring bedding
May	spring bedding, rhododendrons
Jun	rhododendrons
Jul	sumer bedding, roses, herbaceous borders
Aug	summer bedding, roses, herbaceous borders
Sep	roses, herbaceous borders
Oct	autumn colour
Win	snowdrops

Disley, Stockport, Cheshire
SK12 2NX
Tel 01663 762023/766492
Fax 01663 765035
Email lymepark@ntrust.org.uk

Location (7:L7) Entrance on A6, 6½ml SE of Stockport, 9ml NW of Buxton (house and car park 1ml from entrance) [109:SJ965825]

Soil Acid clay/loam

Terrain Split level with ravine

Altitude 245m/804ft

Area 6.8 hectares/17 acres

Gardeners 5 full-time

Great gardeners Graham Stuart Thomas

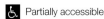 Partially accessible

Scented plants, guide dogs allowed

Events Guided walks, Theatre in the Garden, Teddy Bears' Picnic

Other gardens in the area
Dunham Massey
Hare Hill
Tatton Park
Arley Hall (not NT)
Chatsworth (not NT)
Dunge Valley Garden (not NT)

A colourful oasis in an otherwise rugged landscape in the foothills of the Pennines. Represents 600 years of ownership by the Legh family, but largely restored to its mid-Victorian splendour, with bold spring and summer bedding schemes in the sunken parterre and on the formal terraces. While the formal panel beds display annuals, including *Penstemon* 'Rubicundus', first raised at Lyme in 1906, the long border below the orangery terrace is planted with perennials following a scheme drawn up by Graham Stuart Thomas in 1966. The orangery, designed by Lewis Wyatt, contains camellias that were probably introduced in the 1860s.

The superbly presented Edwardian rose garden was restored in 1995, and the programme continued with restoration of the 'English Garden', based on Wyatt's early 19th-century design with period plants, completed in 2001. Paths suitable for wheelchair users and pushchairs have recently been laid.

A Victorian bedding scheme in front of Lewis Wyatt's conservatory (NTPL/Geoff Morgan)

Lytes Cary Manor

Charming Somerset manor house inhabited by the Lyte family from the 13th to 18th centuries. Henry Lyte's *Nieuwe Herbal* – a translation from a Flemish work – was dedicated to Queen Elizabeth I. The property was neglected after the Lyte family left in 1748 but was rescued by Sir Walter Jenner who bought it in 1907. Sir Walter created a wonderful garden divided by clipped yew hedges, with colourful shrubs, roses and a herbaceous border. A raised walk overlooking the orchard is planted with crab apples, medlar, quince and spring bulbs. A yew-hedged walk leads to a formal pool with statues of Flora and Diana. Hornbeam tunnel leads to crescent of variegated weigela.

Apr	orchard, spring bulbs
May	topiary, lawns
Jun	roses, geranium, lilies, honeysuckle
Jul	cosmos, nicotiana, echinops
Aug	hydrangeas, salvia, caryopteris
Sep	borders, topiary
Oct	borders, topiary
Win	closed

nr Charlton Mackrell, Somerton, Somerset TA11 7HU
Tel/Fax 01458 224471
Email lytescarymanor@ntrust.org.uk

Location (1:J6) Signposted from Podimore roundabout at junction of A303, A37 take A372 [183: ST529269]

Soil Heavy, limy soil

Terrain Level

Altitude 61m/200ft

Area 1.6 hectares/4 acres

Gardeners 1 full-time, 1 part-time

Great gardeners Graham Stuart Thomas

 Fully accessible

 Guide dogs allowed

Plant sales Yes

Other gardens in the area
Barrington Court
Montacute
Stourhead
Tintinhull
East Lambrook Manor (not NT)
Hadspen House (not NT)
Melbury House (not NT)
Milton Lodge Gardens (not NT)

P 👤 👤

Clipped yew hedges designed by Sir Walter Jenner
(NTPL/Stephen Robson)

Melford Hall

Apr	spring flowers
May	irises in dry moat, Judas tree
Jun	herbaceous border
Jul	herbaceous border
Aug	herbaceous border, agapanthus
Sep	
Oct	autumn colour
Win	closed

Set in the confines of what was a medieval moated site, the garden is Edwardian in design. Clipped box hedges and topiary and some fine specimen trees, including two copper beeches and an old mulberry tree. There is a long herbaceous border and a pleasant walk along a dry moat, together with a rare example of a Tudor banqueting house.

Long Melford, Sudbury, Suffolk
CO10 9AA
Tel 01787 880286
Email melford@ntrust.org.uk

Location (4:H7) In Long Melford off A134, 14ml S of Bury St Edmunds, 3ml N of Sudbury [155: TL867462]

Soil Silty loam

Terrain Low-lying valley

Altitude 30m/98ft

Area 1 hectare/2 acres

Gardeners 1 part-time

Partially accessible, (some steps/slopes)

Guide dogs allowed

Other gardens in the area
Kentwell Hall (not NT)
Sun House Garden, Long
  Melford (not NT)

Right: The Octagon pavilion, a little Tudor banqueting house (NTPL/Rupert Truman)

Opposite: 18th-century stone cartouche with the arms of the Mompesson and Longueville families (NTPL/Nick Meers)

Mompesson House

Intimate and sheltered garden enclosed by cathedral wall, house and outbuildings. The garden is based on the design of a central lawn surrounded by paths and herbaceous borders containing a wide variety of plants, mostly replanted by the NT since 1975. Features include a pergola covered in wistaria, honeysuckle and clematis. In the cathedral close wall is a small panelled room, once perhaps a privy. Lavender Walk, paved sitting area and garden tea room. Scented plants include old roses, *Trachelospermum asiaticum* and, at the front of the house, *Magnolia grandiflora* and myrtle. Trees include *Magnolia x soulangeana* and *Koelreuteria paniculata*. Essentially a traditional English garden of great charm.

Apr	magnolias, tulips
May	
Jun	roses, herbaceous borders
Jul	roses, herbaceous borders
Aug	herbaceous borders
Sep	herbaceous borders
Oct	
Win	closed

The Close, Salisbury, Wiltshire SP1 2EL
Tel 01722 335659
Fax 01722 321559
Email mompessonhouse@ntrust.org.uk

Location (1:L5) On N side of Choristers' Green in the Cathedral Close, near High Street Gate [184: SU142295]

Soil Alkaline, light soil

Terrain Level, sheltered and walled

Altitude 20m/66ft

Area 0.2 hectares/0.5 acres

Gardeners 1 part-time

 Fully accessible

 Scented plants, guide dogs allowed

Other gardens in the area
Stourhead Landscape Garden
Wilton House (not NT)

Monk's House

Apr	spring bulbs
May	spring bulbs
Jun	herbaceous
Jul	herbaceous
Aug	herbaceous
Sep	herbaceous
Oct	
Win	closed

Rodmell, Lewes, Sussex
BN7 3HF
Tel 0870 458 4000

Location (2:G8) From A27 SW of
Lewes, follow signs for Kingston
and then Rodmell village, where
turn left at Abergavenny Arms
pub, thence ½ml
[198: TQ421064]

Monk's House was the home of Leonard and Virginia
Woolf from 1919 and the garden is still largely as it was
in the Woolfs' time. Near the house yew hedges, paths
and flintstone walls from an old piggery frame formal
herbaceous areas. The orchard leads to the bowling
green and dew-pond. The garden-room, where
Virginia used to work, still contains her writing desk,
and there is a display of photographs with extracts
from her diaries and letters.

Soil Alkaline, medium-light soil

Terrain Low-lying level ground in
Ouse Valley

Altitude 15m/49ft

Area 0.5 hectares/1 acre

Gardeners 1 part-time

Not suitable for wheelchairs

Scented plants, guide dogs
allowed

Other gardens in the area
Sheffield Park
Charleston Farmhouse (not NT)

View of the garden, looking towards Leonard Woolf's conservatory
(NTPL/David Sellman)

Montacute House

The garden follows the original Elizabethan layout but with 19th- and 20th-century additions. Raised walks frame a sunken lawn encircled by clipped yew and American hawthorn with a 19th-century pond at its centre. Borders of shrub roses under the retaining wall include 16th-century species such as *Rosa gallica officinalis* and *R.* 'Alba Maxima' planted on the advice of Vita Sackville-West. Phyllis Reiss, from nearby Tintinhull, chose the strong colour schemes for the border in the East Court which includes herbaceous perennials, standard honeysuckles, clematis and vines, and contrasts well with the honey-coloured stone of the house. The West Drive, created in 1851, is lined with cedars and fronted by clipped Irish yews.

A new education area with interpretation, including Somerset apples, coppicing and bees, will be opening in 2002.

Apr	topiary
May	early fig walk, border
Jun	mixed herbaceous border
Jul	roses
Aug	mixed herbaceous border
Sep	mixed herbaceous border
Oct	orangery, topiary
Win	closed

Montacute, Somerset TA15 6XP
Tel/Fax 01935 823289
Email montacute@ntrust.org.uk

Location (1:J6) In Montacute village, 4ml W of Yeovil, on S side of A3088, 3ml E of A303; signposted
[183 & 193: ST499172]

Soil Alkaline/sandy silt loam, some clay

Terrain Flat

Altitude 75m/246ft

Area 5 hectares/12 acres

Gardeners 3 + 1 careership full-time

Great gardeners Phyllis Reiss, Vita Sackville-West, Graham Stuart Thomas

Partially accessible

Scented plants, guide dogs allowed

Other gardens in the area
Barrington Court
Lytes Cary
Tintinhull
Lambrook Manor (not NT)

16th-century balustrades of the East Court providing a mellow backdrop to the summer borders (NTPL/Neil Campbell-Sharp)

Moseley Old Hall

Apr	primroses, spring bulbs
May	bulbs, blossom
Jun	old roses
Jul	lavender, honeysuckle, clematis
Aug	clematis, grapevine
Sep	herbaceous plants
Oct	medlars
Win	snowdrops

Moseley Old Hall Lane,
Fordhouses, Wolverhampton,
Staffordshire WV10 7HY
Tel/Fax 01902 782808
Email
moseleyoldhall@ntrust.org.uk

Location (6:D6) 4ml N of
Wolverhampton; S of M54
between A449 and A460; traffic
from N on M6 leave motorway at
exit 11, then A460; traffic from S
on M6 & M54 take exit 1;
coaches must approach via
A460 to avoid low bridge
[127: SJ932044]

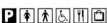

Soil Heavy neutral

Terrain Flat, fairly sheltered

Altitude 75m/246ft

Area 0.5 hectares/1 acre

Gardeners 2 part-time

♿ Fully accessible

♿ Scented plants, guide dogs
allowed

Events Garden tours 3rd Sunday
of month

Other gardens in the area
Wightwick Manor

A small 17th-century-style garden planted with period herbs, fruits and flowering plants. The main feature is a knot garden that follows one of five designs laid out by the Rev. Walter Stonehouse, Rector of Darfield in Yorkshire in 1640. Other features include the nut alley, lined on either side with different varieties of hazel, the vine- and clematis-covered arbour, the herb garden and the orchard which has 17th-century varieties of fruit trees. Mixed borders of shrubs, plants, herbs and roses of old European origin, such as the Red Rose of Lancaster (*Rosa gallica officinalis*), make a delightful mixture of the formal and the natural.

The knot garden, laid out in 17th-century style with dwarf box trees.
(NTPL/Nick Meers)

Mottisfont Abbey

River valley garden of lawn, specimen trees and woodland laid out around the remains of a medieval priory, and including features designed by Geoffrey Jellicoe and Norah Lindsay. A naturally-occurring spring, or font, feeds into a tributary of the River Test.

The former kitchen garden contains the National Collection of Shrub Roses (pre-1900), laid out by Graham Stuart Thomas in the 1970s and 1980s. Echoing the kitchen garden layout, he arranged the rose beds in four large plots with an outer boxed walk. The borders are planted with herbaceous plants chosen to complement the roses and extend the flowering season.

Apr	bulbs, magnolias
May	magnolias, roses
Jun	roses
Jul	herbaceous borders
Aug	hardy annuals, clematis
Sep	clematis, roses
Oct	trees, autumn colour
Win	closed

Mottisfont, nr Romsey,
Hampshire SO51 0LP
Tel 01794 340757
Fax 01794 341492
Email
mottisfontabbey@ntrust.org.uk

Soil Alkaline

Terrain Level, river valley

Altitude 45m/148ft

Area 10.5 hectares/26 acres

Gardeners 4 full-time, 1 seasonal

Great gardeners Graham Stuart Thomas, Norah Lindsay, Geoffrey Jellicoe

 Partially accessible

Braille guide, scented plants, guide dogs allowed

Plant sales Home-grown plants always for sale, roses: Mar–Jul

Events Late May plant fair, programmed guided walks – seasonal, 'Rose Clinic' evenings in June

Other gardens in the area
Hinton Ampner
Hillier Arboretum, Romsey (not NT)
Houghton Lodge, Hydroponics (not NT)
Longstock Water Garden (not NT)

Location (2:C7) 4½ml NW of Romsey, 1ml W of A3057 [185: SU327270]

Rosa Complicata Gallica, one of the collection of old roses at Mottisfont (NTPL/Andrea Jones)

Mottistone Manor

Apr	blossom
May	bluebells
Jun	kitchen garden
Jul	herbaceous borders
Aug	herbaceous borders
Sep	orchard
Oct	autumn colour
Win	closed

The Gardener, Manor Cottage,
Hoxall Lane, Mottistone, Isle of
Wight PO30 4ED
Tel 01983 741302

Location (2:C9) At Mottistone,
2ml W of Brighstone on B3399
[196: SZ406838]

Soil Sandy soil, neutral

Terrain Small valley, with coastal
views

Altitude 60m/197ft

Area 2 hectares/5 acres

Gardeners 2 full-time

  Partially accessible, (steep
slopes)

  Scented plants, guide dogs
allowed

Plant sales Every open day

Events Spring garden fair, Easter
egg hunt, regular programme of
guided walks, jazz concerts
beginning of August

Other gardens in the area
Morton Manor (not NT)
Osborne House (not NT)
Ventnor Botanic Gardens
(not NT)

Tranquil, south-facing valley garden with grassy terraces planted with trees and shrubs, with fine coastal views. The planting has a Mediterranean theme, with shrub borders, herbaceous borders, an organic kitchen garden restored in 2000, and an orchard. There is a tea-garden, with teas served from the summer-house. The garden also contains a unique 1930s hut, known as 'the shack', with Art Deco interior. Architects Seely & Paget built it as their retreat from London.

One of the herbaceous borders (NT/David Sellman)

102

Mount Stewart

This famous garden was created in the 1920s by Edith, wife of the 7th Marquess of Londonderry. Taking advantage of the mild microclimate of the Ards Peninsula, she built up an unrivalled collection of plants, including many rare examples. Features range from the 18th-century Temple of the Winds, designed by James 'Athenian' Stuart as a banqueting house overlooking Strangford Lough, to colourful formal parterres and elaborate topiary. Rhododendrons and exotic trees, including many from the southern hemisphere. Statuary includes the extraordinary Dodo Terrace, with figures representing family and friends of Lady Londonderry.

Apr	rhododendrons, magnolias
May	rhododendrons, magnolias
Jun	rhododendrons, herbaceous borders
Jul	Italian garden
Aug	formal areas
Sep	lake area
Oct	lake area, trees
Win	lake area

Newtownards, Down BT22 2AD
Tel 028 4278 8387/8487
Fax 028 4278 8569
Email mountstewart@ntrust.org.uk

Location (1:K5) 15ml SE of Belfast on Newtownards–Portaferry road, A20, 5ml SE of Newtownards [J553695]

Soil Slightly acid

Terrain Flat and undulating

Altitude sea level

Area approx 32 hectares/79 acres

Gardeners 7 full-time

 Fully accessible

Scented plants, guide dogs allowed

 dogs allowed on leads

Plant sales Annual Garden Fair in May

Events Regular programme of head gardener walks and musical events.

Other gardens in the area
Rowallane

The Dodo Terrace
(NTPL/Stephen Robson)

103

Nostell Priory

Apr	daffodils
May	rhododendrons, magnolias
Jun	herbaceous border
Jul	roses
Aug	roses
Sep	
Oct	autumn colours
Win	closed

Doncaster Road, Nostell, nr
Wakefield, Yorkshire WF4 1QE
Tel 01924 863892
Fax 01924 865282
Email nostellpriory@ntrust.org.uk

Location (8:C8) On the A638
5ml SE of Wakefield towards
Doncaster [111: SE407172]

Shrub and woodland garden centred on an informal lake which dates from at least medieval times. Two designs for the garden, by Joseph Perfect and Stephen Switzer, survive from the 1730s. Some of Switzer's work was carried out but little remains today. Much 19th-century planting of rhododendrons. West of the lake stands a small gothick menagerie designed by Robert Adam. Nearby is a round cockpit, but no traces of original enclosures for animals. Handsome three-arched bridge where road crosses lake. Fine trees. Adventure playground.

Soil Acid, heavy

Terrain Slightly undulating, sheltered valley site

Altitude 61m/200ft

Area 4.8 hectares/12 acres

Gardeners 2 full-time

  Partially accessible

  Guide dogs allowed

Other gardens in the area
Clumber Park
East Riddlesden Hall
Bramham Park (not NT)
Brodsworth Hall (not NT)
Lotherton Hall (not NT)
Yorkshire Sculpture Park (not NT)

The 18th-century bridge (NTPL/Matthew Antrobus)

Nunnington Hall

The walled garden on the banks of the River Rye offers a perfect complement to the mellow 17th-century manor house.

The long mixed borders are planted in an informal cottage style, offering colour and impact throughout the season. Orchards of traditional Ryedale apple varieties and old-fashioned culinary pears border the main lawn in front of the house. The grassland running through the orchards is managed as a wildflower meadow with informal bulb planting to coincide with the apple and cherry blossom.

Formal rose gardens along the south wall were originally planted by the donor family and there is a unique iris garden in a secluded corner of the garden.

Apr	daffodils, pear blossom
May	wildflower meadows, apple blossom
Jun	iris, roses
Jul	herbaceous borders
Aug	herbaceous borders
Sep	orchard fruit
Oct	autumn colour
Win	closed

Nunnington, York, YO62 5UY
Tel 01439 748283
Fax 01439 748284
Email
nunningtonhall@ntrust.org.uk

Location (8:D5) In Ryedale, 4½ml SE of Helmsley (A170) Helmsley–Pickering road; 1½ml N of B1257 Malton–Helmsley road; 21ml N of York, B1363.
[100: SE670795]

Soil Medium loam

Terrain North-facing slope, sheltered

Altitude 60m/197ft

Area 3.4 hectares/8 acres

Gardeners 1 full-time, 1 part-time

 Partially accessible

Scented plants, guide dogs allowed

Plant sales Annual plant fair and year-round plant sales area

Events Annual garden activities and events programme. Please phone for details.

Other gardens in the area
Beningbrough Hall
Ormesby Hall
Rievaulx Terrace and Temples
Castle Howard (not NT)
Duncombe Park (not NT)
Helmsley (not NT)

The garden in spring (NT)

Nymans Garden

Apr	magnolia, fritillaries, wild orchids
May	rhododendrons, bluebells, wistaria, davidia, embothrium
Jun	roses, herbaceous borders, cornus, deutzia
Jul	summer borders, sunken gardens, standard fuchsias
Aug	summer borders, hydrangeas, gunnera, heather
Sep	eucryphia nymansensis, pampas grass
Oct	autumn colour, heathers, hydrangeas, autumn crocus
Win	snowdrops, snowflakes, pinetum, cyclamen

One of the great gardens of the Sussex Weald, offering a feast of colour throughout the year. Created by the Messel family over three generations from 1890. Originally it was planned around a pastiche '14th-century' manor house that was gutted by fire in 1947, and now forms a picturesque shell.

The Messels intended to display as wide a variety of plants as possible from all over the world, dispatching plant hunters that included Harold, son of their head gardener, James Comber. The result is a magnificent collection of magnolias, rhododendrons, and other flowering trees and shrubs, including plants hybridised at Nymans such as Camellia 'Leonard Messel'.

In high summer the double flower borders are a striking feature, while the garden is open at weekends throughout the winter.

Handcross, nr Haywards Heath, Sussex RH17 6EB
Tel 01444 400321/405250
Fax 01444 400253
Email nymans@ntrust.org.uk

Location (2:G7) On B2114 at Handcross, 4½ml S of Crawley, just off London–Brighton M23/A23 [187: TQ265294]

Soil Fertile, lime-free

Terrain Level

Altitude 150m/492ft

Area 12 (243 incl park) hectares/30254 acres

Gardeners 7 full-time, 1 part-time

Great gardeners James Comber, Roy Lancaster, Martin Gardener

 Partially accessible

Braille guide, scented plants, guide dogs allowed

Events Plant of the Month coffee mornings, lecture lunches & guided walks

Other gardens in the area
Sheffield Park
Standen
Wakehurst Place
Borde Hill Garden (not NT)
High Beeches Garden (not NT)
Leonardslee Gardens (not NT)

Ormesby Hall

The garden is formal in design, with modest terraces of mixed hybrid tea roses and lavender, close-mown lawn and specimen trees. Beds of delphinium, agapanthus and seasonal annuals, house walls part-draped in climbing roses and wistaria. In contrast to this formality, the ash, beech and oak copse is fringed in spring with snowdrops, aconites, daffodils and primroses, and later with cow parsley and aruncus. In the lower part of the west garden, a holly walk and shady ribbon border. Much of the garden's character comes from trees. Limes, chestnuts, crab apples and walnut and fine sycamore and purple beech. Bolstered by evergreen Portugal Laurel, they give a sheltering frame to the exposed site.

Opposite: Magnolia 'Leonard Messel' in the Top Garden (NTPL/Stephen Robson)

Below: The formal garden, with a bed of seasonal annuals (NTPL/David Tarn)

Apr	spring bulbs, blossom
May	blossom
Jun	herbaceous borders, roses
Jul	shrubs, herbaceous borders, roses
Aug	herbaceous borders, roses
Sep	herbaceous borders
Oct	shrubs
Win	aconites, snowdrops, shrubs

Ormesby, Middlesbrough, TS7 9AS
Tel 01642 324188
Fax 01642 300937
Email ormesbyhall@ntrust.org.uk

Location (9:L9) 3ml SE of Middlesbrough, W of A171. From the A19 take the A174 to the A172. Follow signs for Ormesby Hall. Car entrance on Ladgate Lane (B1380) [93: NZ530167]

Soil Alkaline/heavy clay

Terrain Level, some steps

Altitude 47m/154ft

Area 2 hectares/5 acres

Gardeners 1 full-time

Fully accessible

Braille guide, scented plants, guide dogs allowed

Plant sales In shop

Events Plant fair, tours with the gardener, tree walk day

Other gardens in the area
Nunnington Hall
Rievaulx Terrace and Temples
Helmsley Walled Garden (not NT)

Osterley Park

Apr	interest all season
May	interest all season
Jun	interest all season
Jul	interest all season
Aug	interest all season
Sep	interest all season
Oct	interest all season
Win	interest all season

Jersey Road, Isleworth, London
(Hounslow) TW7 4RB
Tel 020 8232 5050
Fax 020 8232 5080
Email osterley@ntrust.org.uk

Location (3:F5) Follow brown
tourist signs on A4 between
Gillette Corner and Osterley
underground station (access via
Thornbury Rd & Jersey Rd); M4,
Jn 3 [176: TQ146780]

Soil Lime-free, gravel, clay

Terrain Level

Altitude 30m/98ft

Area 58 hectares/143 acres

Gardeners 5 full-time, 1 part-time,
1 seasonal

Fully accessible

Guide dogs allowed

On leads only

Events NGS open day June.
Phone the property for full details

Other gardens in the area
Cliveden
Fenton House
Ham House
Syon Park (not NT)

A tranquil oasis in the heart of London, Osterley's
18th-century landscaped park, with its ornamental
lakes and formal pleasure grounds surrounded by
farmland, surprises and delights the visitor. Given to
the NT in 1949 by the 9th Earl of Jersey. Well known
for its fine specimen trees, particularly oaks, including
Quercus cerris and *Quercus frainetto*, the Turkey and
Hungarian oaks, and hickories. A ten-year project to
recreate the essence of the 'Gardenesque' style in the
pleasure grounds is nearing completion. Interesting
garden buildings include temple and semi-circular
garden house by Robert Adam. Waymarked estate walk
($2\frac{1}{2}$miles).

On NGS days only, visitors may see the Cutting
Garden, which provides 18th-century-style flowers for
the house.

The garden lake in winter (NTPL/Ian Shaw)

Overbecks Garden

Otto Overbeck created a Mediterranean garden on a magnificent site overlooking the Salcombe Estuary. In a letter written in 1933, he rhapsodised 'It is so warm and beautiful here. I grow Bananas, Oranges, and Pomegranates in the open garden, and have 3,000 palm trees, planted out in my woods and garden'. Informal and adventurous in spirit, the garden is a blaze of colour in summer – in particular in July and August – with beds combining herbaceous plants with pots and urns containing agaves.

Unlike many West Country gardens, Overbecks does not rely on rhododendrons and camellias because of the alkaline soil. Instead, the old and famous *Magnolia campbellii* provide a wonderful sight in early spring.

Apr	unusual bulbs
May	Mediterranean shrubs
Jun	bananas
Jul	tender perennials
Aug	tender perennials
Sep	tender perennials
Oct	autumn colour
Win	magnolias

Sharpitor, Salcombe, Devon
TQ8 8LW
Tel 01548 842893
Fax 01548 844038
Email overbecks@ntrust.org.uk

Location (1:F9) 1½ml SW of Salcombe, signposted from Malborough and Salcombe (narrow approach road) [202: SX728374]

Soil Slightly alkaline

Terrain Terraced cliffside

Altitude 30m/98ft

Area 2.4 hectares/6 acres

Gardeners 2 full-time

 Partially accessible

 Scented plants, guide dogs allowed

Plant sales Plant fair in May

Events Guided walks, phone for details

Other gardens in the area
Coleton Fishacre
Greenway
Saltram

Agapanthus, canna and kniphofias with palm trees
(NTPL/Mark Bolton)

Oxburgh Hall

Apr	spring flowers
May	spring flowers
Jun	parterre, herbaceous border
Jul	parterre, herbaceous border
Aug	herbaceous border
Sep	
Oct	autumn colour
Win	closed

Oxborough, King's Lynn, Norfolk
PE33 9PS
Tel 01366 328258
Fax 01366 328066
Email oxburghhall@ntrust.org.uk

Location (4:G4) At Oxborough,
7ml SW of Swaffham on S side
of Stoke Ferry road
[143: TF742012]

The parterre, laid out in Victorian
times, but based on an early 18th-
century design
(NTPL/Matthew Antrobus)

Moated house built in 1482 by the Bedingfeld family.
Lawns fringed with fine trees. The Victorian parterre
planted by Sir Henry Paston-Bedingfeld, *c*.1845, is in
the French 18th-century style with some permanent
plantings, of blue rue and *Cineraria maritima* 'Silver
Dust', together with seasonal plantings of *Geranium*
'Paul Crampel', marigolds and ageratum. The violet
and yellow of the scheme are reversed each year.

The Victorian kitchen garden is now planted as a
formal orchard with plum, medlar, quince and gage,
while roses and clematis grow on the walls. The long
herbaceous border behind the yew hedge is very fine
in summer. There is also a beautifully restored
vegetable garden.

Soil Limy

Terrain Level

Altitude 30m/98ft

Area 7.5 hectares/19 acres

Gardeners 2 full-time, 1 part-time

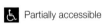 Partially accessible

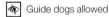 Guide dogs allowed

Events Meet the Gardener
(monthly), garden tours by
arrangement

Packwood House

Grade II* listed with famous yew garden said to represent the Sermon on the Mount, originally set out by John Fetherston *c*.1650-70. A large single yew set on a tall mound is reached by a spiral path, with 12 large yews on the terrace below. Many more, representing the Multitude, were planted below in the 1850s in what was once an orchard. The 17th-century terraced raised walk is reached via semi-circular brick steps with an 18th-century wrought iron gate at the top. Set into the wall on one side are bee boles for housing woven bee hives. Carolean garden beside the house enclosed by 17th-century brick walls with gazebos at each corner. Fine herbaceous borders along walls of the Carolean garden, in the raised garden and around sunken pool. Roman baths and sundials.

Apr	wall shrubs
May	sunken garden, tulips
Jun	borders
Jul	borders
Aug	yellow border, raised terrace, herbaceous and bedding
Sep	raised terrace, tender perennials
Oct	
Win	closed

Lapworth, Solihull, Warwickshire B94 6AT
Tel 01564 783294
Fax 01564 782706
Email packwood@ntrust.org.uk

Location (6:E7) 2ml E of Hockley Heath (on A3400), 11ml SE of central Birmingham
[139: SP174722]

Soil Alkaline

Terrain Gently sloping exposed site

Altitude 120m/394ft

Area 2.8 hectares/7 acres

Gardeners 3 full-time, 1 seasonal

Partially accessible

Guide dogs allowed

Plant sales Spring Plant Fair

Events Meet the Gardener (twice a year)

Other gardens in the area
Baddesley Clinton
Charlecote Park
Coughton Court
Farnborough Hall
Upton House
Castle Bromwich (not NT)

The Carolean garden, looking towards the gazebo, with kniphofias in the foreground (NTPL/Stephen Robson)

111

Peckover House

Apr	daffodils, tulips
May	roses, tulips
Jun	roses, borders
Jul	borders
Aug	borders
Sep	autumn colours, red border
Oct	autumn colours
Win	closed

North Brink, Wisbech,
Cambridgeshire PE13 1JR
Tel/Fax 01945 583463
Email peckover@ntrust.org.uk

Location (4:F3) On N bank of
River Nene, in Wisbech (B1441)
[143: TF458097]

Outstanding Victorian garden of a Georgian house
originally owned by a Quaker banking family. Spacious
lawns shaded by specimen trees including gingko,
Chusan palm, Tulip and monkey puzzle. Eastern edge
of garden planted with laurels, hollies, box and yew,
forming a wilderness area.

The orangery contains fruit-bearing trees, as well as
colourful displays of pot plants throughout the year,
especially in spring. Other features include elegant
summer-houses, roses, herbaceous borders, ribbon
borders, a Victorian fernery, croquet lawn and a reed
barn. Double herbaceous borders were designed by
Graham Stuart Thomas. The propagation house is open
to the public.

Soil Rich alluvial soil

Terrain Level

Altitude 30m/98ft

Area 0.8 hectares/2 acres

Gardeners 1 full-time

Great gardeners Graham Stuart
Thomas

Partially accessible

Scented plants, guide dogs
allowed

Other gardens in the area
Sandringham House (not NT)

The double herbaceous borders
(NTPL/Stephen Robson)

Penrhyn Castle

Penrhyn is set against dramatic views of the mountains of Snowdonia and the Menai Strait. Surrounded by pleasure grounds and woodland, the garden contains many fine examples of native and exotic trees, vast drifts of snowdrops, daffodils, bluebells, and varied wildflower areas. The formal and secluded walled garden, dating from the Victorian era, contains terraces of parterre design, and below 'Gardenesque' areas of trees and shrubs. The whole site is planted with diverse exotic species offering all-year-round interest.

Apr	bulbs, magnolias, rhododendrons
May	rhododendrons, bluebells
Jun	wild flowers
Jul	fuchsias
Aug	eucryphias
Sep	fuchsias
Oct	autumn colour
Win	snowdrops

Bangor, Gwynedd LL57 4HN
Tel 01248 353084
Fax 01248 371281
Email penrhyncastle@ntrust.org.uk

Location (0:F2) 1ml E of Bangor, at Llandygai on A5122. Signposted from junction of A55 and A5 [115: SH602720]]

The fuchsia arch (NTPL/Stephen Robson)

Soil Neutral/sandy, stony

Terrain Steep sloping site exposed to prevailing winds

Altitude 46m/151ft

Area 19.5 hectares/48 acres

Gardeners 3 full-time, 1 part-time, 2 seasonal plus volunteers

Great gardeners Walter Speed

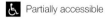 Partially accessible

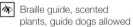 Braille guide, scented plants, guide dogs allowed

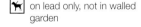 on lead only, not in walled garden

Events Guided walks by appointment

Other gardens in the area
Bodnant
Plas Newydd
Plas Yn Rhiw

113

Petworth House

Apr	daffodils, wild flowers, blossom
May	bluebells, wild flowers
Jun	azaleas, wild flowers
Jul	
Aug	
Sep	
Oct	
Win	closed

Petworth, Sussex GU28 0AE
Tel 01798 342207
Fax 01798 342963
Email petworth@ntrust.org.uk

Location (2:F7) In centre of Petworth (A272/A283); house car park well signposted, car parks for house and park on A283; pedestrian access from Petworth town and from A272. No vehicles in park [197: SU976218]

Capability Brown landscaped deer park with two lakes, tree-crowned hills and peripheral plantations, immortalised in J.M.W. Turner's paintings. The woodland garden, with its Doric temple and Ionic rotunda, enclosed by a ha-ha, was inspired by Brown, who also enriched the planting with exotic species of trees and shrubs. The diversity of habitat supports a wide range of plants, with the tradition of adventurous planting continued to the present day. Lovely wild-flower meadows and excellent views over the surrounding countryside.

Soil Greensand over stone, acid

Terrain Hilly

Altitude Average 65m/213ft

Area 283.5 hectares/701 acres

Gardeners 4 full-time

Great gardeners George London, Capability Brown

Partially accessible

Guide dogs allowed

Plant sales Spring Plant Fair in May

Events Occasional guided tours, open-air concerts, Kite Festival

Other gardens in the area
Nymans
Uppark
Denmans (not NT)
Parham Park (not NT)
West Dean (not NT)

The Ionic rotunda in the pleasure grounds (NTPL/David Sellman)

Plas Newydd

A parkland garden with formal terraces, shrub beds and trees, based on a Humphry Repton design and developed by the present Marquess of Anglesey since the 1950s and by the NT since 1976. In spring the azaleas and magnolias, wild rhododendron garden and Australasian arboretum with shrub understorey are complemented by local wild flowers. Summer-flowering shrubs include escallonia, olearia and hoheria. The Terrace Garden features hot and cool borders in July and August, with pools and fountains. Hydrangeas, acers and azaleas provide good autumn colour. The garden offers marine and woodland walks, with spectacular views of Snowdonia.

Apr	azaleas, magnolias
May	cherry blossom, azaleas, rhododendrons
Jun	wild flowers
Jul	arboretum, wild flowers
Aug	hydrangeas
Sep	hydrangeas, eucryphia
Oct	autumn colour, hydrangeas
Win	closed

Llanfairpwll, Anglesey, LL61 6DQ
Tel 01248 714795
Fax 01248 713673
Email plasnewydd@ntrust.org.uk

Location (0:E2) 2ml SW of Llanfairpwll and A5 on A4080 to Brynsiencyn; turn off A5 at W end of Britannia Bridge [114/115: SH521696]

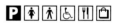

Soil Acid with some alkaline areas – clay and sandstone overlying limestone

Terrain East-sloping with tree shelter from west wind

Altitude 30m/98ft

Area 20 hectares/49 acres

Gardeners 4 full-time, 1 seasonal

Great gardeners Humphry Repton

♿ Partially accessible

🐕 Scented plants, guide dogs allowed

Events Plant fair, guided walks by arrangement

Other gardens in the area
Bodnant
Penrhyn Castle

The Italianate Terrace Garden (NTPL/Nick Meers)

Plas Yn Rhiw

Apr	rhododendrons
May	rhododendrons, camellias, magnolias, wistaria
Jun	wild flowers
Jul	herbaceous beds
Aug	herbaceous beds, eucryphias
Sep	hydrangeas
Oct	woodland colour
Win	snowdrops, magnolias

Rhiw, Pwllheli, Gwynedd
LL53 8AB
Tel/Fax 01758 780219

Location (0:D4) 16 ml from
Pwllheli. Approach route
changed due to landslip. Follow
A499 and B4413 from Pwllheli.
At Botwnnog, follow signs to
Plas yn Rhiw along narrow lanes
past Rhiw village. Entrance at
bottom of steep hill.
[123: SH237282]

Soil Medium loam, slight acid to
neutral,alkaline pockets

Terrain Steep hillside

Altitude 30m/98ft

Area 0.3 hectares/1 acre

Gardeners 1 full-time

 Partially accessible

 Scented plants, guide dogs
allowed

Plant sales Spring plant fair

Events Snowdrop weekends,
guided walk with the gardener

Other gardens in the area
Penrhyn Castle
Plas Newydd
Plas Brondanw (not NT)
Plas Nanhoron (not NT)
Plas Tan-y-Bwlch (not NT)
Portmeirion (not NT)

These ornamental gardens, rescued from neglect and partly redesigned from 1938 by the three Keating sisters, lie at the foot of Mynydd Rhiw mountain, which provides a microclimate enabling many exotic flowering trees and shrubs to flourish. Herbaceous beds, characteristically overplanted, are woven together by a maze of box-framed paths. Ruins of a stable, dairy and housemaids' quarters are landscaped into the garden. The inclusion of many indigenous wild flowers embellishes the wild, romantic setting. A wildflower meadow behind the house borders a native woodland with brilliant displays of snowdrops and bluebells. The garden is managed organically in accordance with the practice of the Misses Keating. Ruined mill. Spectacular views over Hell's Mouth.

Polesden Lacey

The Polesden Lacey estate was left to the National Trust in 1942 by Mrs Ronnie Greville, the renowned society hostess. The gardens, Mrs Greville's creation, are Edwardian in style, with a walled rose garden and separate lavender, iris and peony gardens. The herbaceous border was designed by Graham Stuart Thomas to replace an older planting. Other features include Mrs Greville's collection of statuary and garden ornaments, a croquet lawn and a rock garden.

The gardens are set within 12 ha (30 acres) of lawns from which there are magnificent views over the surrounding countryside.

Apr	
May	bluebells, cowslips
Jun	roses, iris
Jul	roses, herbaceous borders
Aug	roses, herbaceous borders
Sep	
Oct	autumn colour
Win	winter garden, flowering bulbs

Great Bookham, nr Dorking,
Surrey RH5 6BD
Tel 01372 452048
Fax 01372 452023
Email
polesdenlacey@ntrust.org.uk

Soil Light alkaline soil over chalk

Terrain Gentle north-south slope on hilltop site

Altitude 91m/299ft

Area 12 hectares/30 acres

Gardeners 6 full-time

Great gardeners Graham Stuart Thomas

 Partially accessible

 Braille guide, scented plants, guide dogs allowed, (Braille guide in house)

Plant sales At shop throughout summer

Events Guided walks, annual open-air festival second half June, open days, croquet coaching in summer

Other gardens in the area
Clandon Park
Claremont
Hatchlands
Painshill Park (not NT)
Wisley RHS (not NT)

Location (2:F6) 5ml NW of Dorking, 2ml S of Great Bookham, off A246 Leatherhead–Guildford road [187: TQ136522]

Opposite: The box-hedged garden looking towards Hell's Mouth Bay (NTPL/Martin Trelawny)

Right: The Edwardian rose garden (NTPL/Nick Meers)

Powis Castle

Apr	bulbs
May	rhododendron, azaleas, wistaria, laburnum
Jun	roses, clematis
Jul	herbaceous borders, containers
Aug	herbaceous borders, hydrangeas
Sep	herbaceous borders, berried shrubs
Oct	acers, autumn colour
Win	closed

Welshpool, Powys SY21 8RF
Tel 01938 551920
Fax 01938 554336
Email powiscastle@ntrust.org.uk

Location (0:H5) 1ml S of Welshpool; pedestrian access from High Street (A490); cars turn right 1ml along main road to Newtown (A483); enter by first drive gate on right
[126: SJ216064]

Soil Medium heavy loam, ranging from acid to alkaline

Terrain Terraces and steep slopes

Altitude 75mm/246ft

Area 10 hectares/25 acres

Gardeners 8 full-time, 3 seasonal

Great gardeners William Emes, Graham Stuart Thomas

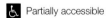 Partially accessible

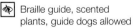 Braille guide, scented plants, guide dogs allowed

Plant sales Thoughout the open season, contact property for details

The garden was first laid out at the end of the 17th century, based on formal designs attributed to William Winde. Notable features remaining are the broad hanging terraces, richly planted and with shaped giant yew trees. The Italianate terraces were inspired by those of the palace at St Germain-en-Laye near Paris, where the 1st Marquess of Powis joined James II in exile in 1689. On the terrace above the Orangery are fine lead urns and statuary by van Nost's workshop, in front of deeply recessed brick alcoves of the aviary. The late 18th-century changes to the garden following the English landscape style are attributed to William Emes. There are many microclimates within the garden, and advantage was taken to develop the ornamental plantings during the 19th and 20th centuries. The kitchen garden was transformed into a formal flower garden in 1911 by Lady Violet, wife of the 4th Earl of Powis. Unusual and tender plants and climbers now prosper in the shelter of high walls and dense hedges. This garden is very steep but well worth the effort as the views are superb.

Events Guided walks with head gardener, demonstrations by garden staff

Other gardens in the area
The Dingle (not NT)
Glansevern Hall Gardens (not NT)

View from the top terrace
(NTPL/Andrew Butler)

Prior Park

A beautiful and intimate 18th-century landscape garden created by local entrepreneur Ralph Allen with advice from the poet Alexander Pope. The garden is set in a sweeping valley with magnificent views of the city of Bath. It includes such ornamental features as the Palladian Bridge, one of only four in the world (and complete with graffiti from the 18th and 19th centuries), the Rock Gate, Sham Bridge, wilderness, rococo grotto and remnants of cascades and the Serpentine Lake. The NT is restoring the garden, using historical, archaeological and ecological surveys. There are also plans to recreate an authentic 18th-century planting style.

Apr	daffodils
May	wild garlic and may blossom
Jun	cherry
Jul	trees
Aug	trees
Sep	trees
Oct	autumn colour from beech and Norway maple
Win	closed until Feb

Ralph Allen Drive, Bath, Bath & NE Somerset BA2 5AH
Tel 01225 833422
Email priorpark@ntrust.org.uk

Location (1:K4) All visitors must use public transport as there is no parking at Prior Park or nearby. To obtain a leaflet explaining how to reach the garden, tel. 01225 833422 [172:ST760633]

Soil Alkaline loam

Terrain Sloping valley

Altitude 90m/295ft

Area 11 hectares/27 acres

Gardeners 2 full-time, 1 part-time

♿ Partially accessible

♿ Braille guide, scented plants, guide dogs allowed, (large print)

Events Guided walks, photo workshop, Easter egg trail, live interpretation, family fun days

Other gardens in the area
The Courts
Dyrham Park
Lacock Abbey
Botanic Garden, Bath (not NT)
Iford Manor (not NT)

The Palladian Bridge, with Bath cityscape behind (NTPL/Joe Cornish)

Rievaulx Terrace and Temples

Apr	primroses
May	cowslips, orchids
Jun	flowering shrubs
Jul	wild flowers
Aug	wild flowers
Sep	
Oct	autumn colour
Win	closed

Rievaulx, Helmsley, York
YO62 5LJ
Tel 01439 798340/01439
748283
Fax 01439 798480

Location (8:D5) 2½ml NW of
Helmsley on B1257
[100: SE579848]

A landscape terrace garden, laid out in 1749 by Thomas
Duncombe II, set high on a hill, overlooking the upper
Rye Valley. The serpentine grass terrace is framed by a
backdrop of woodland and flowering shrub fringe,
with temples – one Ionic, the other Tuscan – situated
at either end. Thirteen vistas cut through the steep
wooded bank offer glimpses of the magnificent ruins
of Rievaulx Abbey and surrounding village. This bank,
designated a Site of Special Scientific Interest,
is managed for its wildlife and plant communities,
notably deadwood invertebrates (no public access).
The adjoining grassy bank is noted for its wild flowers,
of particular interest in May and June with large
numbers of cowslips and early purple orchids. The
backdrop woodland is currently undergoing renovation,
with new tree planting and restoration of the shrub
fringe, recapturing the original 18th-century style.

Soil Thin alkaline

Terrain Level plateau, falling
steeply to west, exposed

Altitude 180m/591ft

Area 24.7 hectares/61 acres

Gardeners 1 full-time, 1 part-time

Fully accessible, (self-drive
vehicle available – please
ring in advance)

Guide dogs allowed

dogs allowed on leads

Events Annual events
programme for all interests.
Please phone for details.

Other gardens in the area
Beningbrough Hall
Nunnington Hall
Ormesby Hall
Castle Howard (not NT)
Duncombe Park (not NT)
Helmsley Walled Garden (not NT)

View along the terrace, towards
the Ionic temple
(NTPL/Andrea Jones)

Rowallane Garden

Although not as formal or as showy as Mount Stewart (page 91), Rowallane is a very beautiful and important garden, often described as a plantsman's garden because of its wonderful collection of plants. It was originally laid out in the mid-19th century, but there were major improvements to the plant collection during the 20th century. All types of gardening are represented here: formal walled and rock gardens, semi-natural and natural landscapes, including managed grassland with large numbers of wild flowers. There is also a unique collection of conifers and an outstanding collection of acid-loving plants.

Apr	rhododendrons
May	azaleas, bulbs, blossom
Jun	shrubs
Jul	roses, fuchsias, herbaceous
Aug	herbaceous, penstemons
Sep	fruit, berries
Oct	autumn colour
Win	early bulbs

Saintfield, Ballynahinch, Down
BT24 7LH
Tel 028 9751 0131
Fax 028 9751 1242
Email rowallane@ntrust.org.uk

Location (1:J6) 11ml SE of Belfast, 1ml S of Saintfield, W of the Downpatrick road (A7) [J412581]

Soil Acid

Terrain Undulating, rocky

Altitude 61m/200ft

Area 21 hectares/52 acres

Gardeners 5 full-time

 Partially accessible

 Scented plants, guide dogs allowed

dogs allowed on leads

Plant sales Annual plant fair, October

Events Varied programme of head gardener walks all year, and musical events

Other gardens in the area
Castle Ward
Mount Stewart
Belfast Botanics (not NT)
Seaforde Gardens (not NT)

Primula rotundifolia 'Rowallane Rose' in the rockery
(NTPL/Stephen Robson)

Rufford Old Hall

Apr	rhododendrons
May	rhododendrons, bluebells
Jun	herbaceous border
Jul	herbaceous border
Aug	herbaceous border
Sep	topiary
Oct	autumn colour
Win	closed

Rufford, nr Ormskirk, Lancashire
L40 1SG
Tel/Fax 01704 821254
Email ruffordoldhall@ntrust.org.uk

Location (7:J5) 7ml N of
Ormskirk, in village of Rufford on
E side of A59 [108: SD463160]

Part of the Leeds and Liverpool
canal which runs through the
garden
(NTPL/Matthew Antrobus)

The layout of the garden is largely Victorian, most of
the existing mature trees and shrubs having been
planted at that time. As well as an abundance of
rhododendrons and azaleas, the garden has woodland
areas, lawns, herbaceous borders and an orchard
featuring old northern varieties of apple. The high wall
of the estate is draped in wistaria. There is some
interesting topiary, including a pair of squirrels, and
19th-century statues of Pan in zinc, and of the infant
Bacchus in lead.

Soil Lime-free sandy loam

Terrain Flat,drained by ditches to
the canal

Altitude 6-10m/20-33ft

Area 5.7 hectares/14 acres

Gardeners 1 full-time

 Partially accessible

 Guide dogs allowed

Events Evenings with the
Gardener, with supper (three
times a year), guided walks,
archery and fencing
demonstrations

Other gardens in the area
Speke Hall
Astley Hall (not NT)
Southport Botanic Gardens
(not NT)

St Michael's Mount

Terraced maritime garden specialising in succulents and tender shrubs. The gardens proper are to be found on the south side of the island and are divided into the east and west terraces and the walled gardens. The terraces were laid out *c.*1900 and are filled with plants mainly from the southern hemisphere such as aloes, agaves, agapanthus and yuccas. The walled gardens were built around 1780 on three levels, the top garden with a summer-house built into the rear wall. These gardens get very hot during the summer and the planting reflects this.

Apr	*Puya chilensis* in flower
May	euryops, calceolaria
Jun	Puya alpestris in flower
Jul	*Actinidia chinensis*
Aug	Begonia Cupensis
Sep	
Oct	
Win	*Sparrmannia africana*

Marazion, nr Penzance, Cornwall
TR17 0EF
Tel 01736 710507
Fax 01736 711544
Email
godolphin@manor-office.co.uk

Location (1:B9) ½ml S of A394 at Marazion, whence there is access on foot over the causeway at low tide or, during summer months only, by ferry at high tide. Tide and ferry information only: tel. 01736 710265/710507
[203: SW515298]

Terraced maritime garden (NT/Rupert Tenison)

Soil Acid

Terrain Steep, very exposed

Altitude 30.5m/100ft

Area 4 hectares/10 acres

Gardeners 3 full-time, 1 seasonal

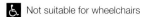 Not suitable for wheelchairs

Scented plants, guide dogs allowed

Plant sales Plant stall

Events Guided tours

Other gardens in the area
Glendurgan
Trengwainton
Probus Gardens (not NT)
Trebah (not NT)

Saltram

Apr	camellias, michelia
May	bluebells, wild flowers, azaleas
Jun	orange grove
Jul	herbaceous border, hydrangeas
Aug	herbaceous border, cyclamen, eucryphias
Sep	herbaceous border
Oct	autumn colour, acers
Win	evergreens, witch hazels, narcissus

Plympton, Plymouth, Devon
PL7 1UH
Tel 01752 333500
Fax 01752 336474
Email saltram@ntrust.org.uk

Location (1:F8) 3½ml E of
Plymouth city centre, between
Plymouth–Exeter road (A38) and
Plymouth–Kingsbridge road
(A379); take Plympton turn at
Marsh Mills roundabout
[201: SX520557]

A plantsman's garden, of interest at all seasons.
Sweeping lawns around the house give way to a
network of paths leading the visitor through the
different areas of the garden. A formal lime avenue,
about 80 yards long, is underplanted with narcissus. In
late summer *Cyclamen hederifolium* carpet the ground.
Rhododendrons, camellias and hydrangeas provide bold
colour amongst the shrubberies, which give shelter to
many interesting plants, including tender species from
the southern hemisphere. Likewise the orange grove,
hidden behind the chapel, offers shelter to tubs of
citrus and agapanthus, giving a Mediterranean flavour.
A herbaceous border designed by Graham Stuart
Thomas offers additional summer colour. Abundant
areas of wild flowers from spring to midsummer. Many
fine specimen trees, notably pines and acers. The
magnificent 18th-century orangery, Gothic castle and
Fanny's Bower provide architectural and historical
interest.

The orange grove
(NTPL/Rupert Truman)

Soil Lime-free

Terrain Undulating hill-top, silt

Altitude 30m/98ft

Area 8.5 hectares/21 acres

Gardeners 3 full-time

Great gardeners Graham Stuart
Thomas

Fully accessible

Scented plants, guide dogs
allowed

Plant sales Plant fair

Other gardens in the area
Antony
Buckland Abbey
Cotehele
The Garden House, Buckland
    Monachorum (not NT)
Lukes Land, Ivybridge (not NT)
Mount Edgcumbe (not NT)

Scotney Castle

One of England's most romantic gardens, designed by the Hussey family in the 1840s in the Picturesque style around the ruins of a 14th-century moated castle. Rhododendrons and azaleas in profusion, with wistaria and roses rambling over old ruins. Features include the Quarry Garden, which is home to many types of fern and heavily scented Ghent azaleas in shades of orange, yellow and cream. The herb garden, designed by Lanning Roper in the 1970s, is a series of semicircular beds, full of fragrant herbs, around a Venetian well-head. The moat, which surrounds the old castle, has along its edge water-loving plants such as yellow iris, rodgersia and kingcups. On the north-west side of the moat is the newly-thatched ice-house. On Pear Tree Island, an isthmus, is a three-piece bronze reclining figure by Henry Moore. Wonderful views and beautiful woodland and estate walks.

Apr	magnolias, spring bulbs
May	Ghent azaleas
Jun	kalmias, rhododendrons
Jul	roses, herbaceous plants
Aug	clematis
Sep	clematis
Oct	autumn colour
Win	spring bulbs

Lamberhurst, Tunbridge Wells, Kent TN3 8JN
Tel 01892 891081
Fax 01892 890110
Email
scotneycastle@ntrust.org.uk

Location (2:H7) 1ml S of Lamberhurst on A21
[188: TQ688353]

Soil Lime free, clay over sandstone

Terrain Slopes, some steep

Altitude 75m/246ft

Area 7.9 hectares/20 acres

Gardeners 4 full-time

Great gardeners Lanning Roper

Fully accessible

Braille guide, scented plants, guide dogs allowed

Events Meet the Gardener Days, Garden Workshops

Other gardens in the area
Bateman's
Sissinghurst Castle
Merriments Gardens (not NT)
Pashley Manor (not NT)

The medieval castle viewed across azaleas and rhododendrons
(NTPL/Stephen Robson)

Shaw's Corner

Apr	daffodils, violets
May	blossom, cowslips
Jun	roses, magnolia
Jul	herbaceous borders, meadow
Aug	sedum, achillea
Sep	asters, vine, orchard
Oct	berries
Win	closed

Ayot St Lawrence, nr Welwyn,
Hertfordshire AL6 9BX
Tel/Fax 01438 820307
Email shawscorner@ntrust.org.uk

Location (4:E8) A1(M) junction 4
or M1 junction 10; follow B653
signed to Wheathamstead, then
The Ayots and Shaw's Corner
[166: TL194167]

Soil Heavy loam

Terrain Mainly level

Altitude 115m/377ft

Area 1.4 hectares/3 acres

Gardeners 1 part-time,
1 seasonal

Partially accessible

Braille guide, scented
plants, guide dogs allowed

Plant sales NGS Day

Events Contact property for list
of events

Other gardens in the area
Gardens of the Rose, St Albans
(not NT)
Hatfield House (not NT)
Knebworth, Jekyll herb garden
(not NT)

Clare Winsten's statue of Saint
Joan emerging from the dell
(NTPL/Matthew Antrobus)

George Bernard Shaw and his wife Charlotte lived
here for over 40 years, and their ashes are scattered
in the garden and around the revolving hut where
Shaw did his writing. Richly planted herbaceous and
shrubbery beds surround the large lawn, orchard and
meadow. All the plants are pre-1950s: traditional plants
such as phlomis, delphinium, lupin, sedum, allium,
achillea, agapanthus, acanthus and aster. Two sets of
rosebeds have been recently recreated, using photographs
taken by Shaw. The garden is mainly self-sufficient,
supported by six compost pits. There is a wooded area
at the bottom of the garden.

Sheffield Park

Magnificent landscaped garden laid out in the 18th century by Capability Brown. It was further developed in the early 20th century by its owner, Arthur Soames, who was responsible for introducing the exciting collection of rare and unusual trees and shrubs, and who provided an inspired planting scheme giving all-year-round colour. Dramatic shows of daffodils and bluebells in spring. Rhododendrons, azaleas, water lilies and the stream garden are spectacular in early summer. Rare trees and shrubs provide splendid autumn colour, and frost adds a touch of magic to winter walks. The four original large lakes linked by waterfalls form the centrepiece and the reflection of the foliage in the water add another dimension to this stunning Grade I garden. Species of special interest include *Gentiana sino-ornata, Sequoiadendron giganteum, Taxodium distichum, Trachycarpus fortunei, Acer palmatum, Amelanchier lamarkii, Nyssa sylvatica, Quercus coccinea, Kalmia latifolia.* Fine collection of hybrid rhododendron and the National Collection of Ghent Azaleas.

Detail of *Picea breweriana* (NTPL/Charlie Waite)

Apr	bluebells
May	rhododendrons, azaleas
Jun	water lilies
Jul	hydrangeas
Aug	lakes
Sep	gentians
Oct	autumn colour
Win	winter walks, spring bulbs

Sheffield Park, Sussex
TN22 3QX
Tel 01825 790231
Fax 01825 791264
Email sheffieldpark@ntrust.org.uk

Location (2:G7) Midway between East Grinstead and Lewes, 5ml NW of Uckfield, on E side of A275 (between A272 & A22), ½ml from Sheffield Park station (Bluebell Rly)
[198: TQ415240]

Soil Heavy clay, lime free pH5.5

Terrain Gently sloping falls to south east

Altitude 91m/299ft

Area 48 hectares/119 acres

Gardeners 4 full-time, 1 seasonal

Great gardeners Capability Brown

♿ Partially accessible

♟ Braille guide, scented plants, guide dogs allowed

Events Guided walks May and October, Early Bird Walk April, Bat Walk July, Fungus Workshop and walk October

Other gardens in the area
Nymans Garden
Wakehurst Place Garden
Borde Hill (not NT)
Leonardslee (not NT)

Shugborough

Apr	daffodils, cherry, spring flowers
May	rhododendrons, azaleas, viburnums
Jun	roses, summer bedding
Jul	roses, herbaceous border
Aug	herbaceous border
Sep	herbaceous border
Oct	herbaceous border, autumn colour
Win	closed

Milford, nr Stafford, ST17 0XB
Tel 01889 881388
Fax 01889 881323

Location (6:D5) Signposted from M6 exit 13; 6ml E of Stafford on A513; entrance at Milford. Pedestrian access from E, from the canal/Little Haywood side of the Estate [127: SJ992225]

Soil Sandy loam

Terrain Level with rising parkland towards Cannock Chase

Altitude 74m/243ft

Area 4 hectares/10 acres

Gardeners 4 full-time

Great gardeners W A Nesfield, (Victorian terraces)

🦽 Fully accessible

🐾 Scented plants, guide dogs allowed

🐕 dogs allowed on leads, in park only

Plant sales Plant fair, July

Other gardens in the area
Dorothy Clive Garden (not NT)
Hodnet Hall (not NT)
Weston Park (not NT)

Landscape and monuments form the structure of these 18th-century Grade I historic gardens. Formal terraces with rhododendrons and superb colour schemes of lavender, yellow roses and grey foliage as well as a Victorian-style rose garden. The temples and monuments which extend onto the adjacent parkland represent a landmark in the evolution of 18th-century landscape, and are among the first neo-Greek style buildings in England.

There are many attractive mature trees, expecially cedar, beech, oak, chestnut and yew. The 'Great Yew' is a 600-year-old single tree with many layered branches covering half an acre. From the gardens there are excellent views of the parkland and its monuments. A long-term planting scheme is taking place to return the parkland to its original woodland landscape with large blocks of native hardwood trees.

Classical monuments and the west front of the mansion, from Nicholas Dall's painting of Shugborough, 1768 (NTPL/John Hammond)

Sissinghurst Castle

The magical creation of Vita Sackville-West and Harold Nicolson, who moved here in 1930 and transformed the ruins of an Elizabethan mansion and its surroundings. The garden was divided into a series of compartments and each 'room' filled with an inspired and informal arrangement of plants around a theme: the White Garden, the Purple Border, the Rose Garden, the Herb Garden, the Lime Walk and the Cottage Garden. The White Garden shows Vita Sackville-West's sensitivity to colour and has inspired countless imitations. *Rosa mulliganii* erupts into a cascade of white flowers in summer, surrounded by numerous other plants with grey foliage and white blossoms. Other areas show the same ingenuity of planting. This combination of formal design and romantic planting has provided a major influence on garden design.

Apr	bulbs, spring flowers
May	iris, late spring flowers
Jun	roses, herbaceous borders
Jul	herbaceous borders, shrubs
Aug	herbaceous borders
Sep	tender perennials, late herbaceous plants
Oct	autumn colour
Win	closed

Sissinghurst, nr Cranbrook, Kent TN17 2AB
Tel 01580 710700
Fax 01580 710702
Email sissinghurst@ntrust.org.uk

Location (2:J7) 2ml NE of Cranbrook, 1ml E of Sissinghurst village (A262) [188: TQ8138]

Soil Clay, neutral pH

Terrain Flat

Altitude 50m/164ft

Area 2.5 hectares/6 acres

Gardeners 7 full-time

Great gardeners Vita Sackville-West, Harold Nicolson

[&] Partially accessible

[♿] Braille guide, scented plants, guide dogs allowed

Other gardens in the area
Scotney Castle
Great Dixter (not NT)

The Tower, from the White Garden
(NTPL/Andrew Lawson)

Sizergh Castle

Apr	spring flowers, ferns
May	spring flowers, ferns
Jun	roses, ferns
Jul	roses, herbaceous borders, ferns
Aug	herbaceous borders, ferns
Sep	autumn colour, ferns
Oct	autumn colour, ferns
Win	closed

Sizergh, nr Kendal, Cumbria
LA8 8AE
Tel 015395 60070
Fax 015395 61621
Email
Ntrust@sizerghcastle.fsnet.co.uk

Location (7:D7) 3½ml S of
Kendal, signposted off A590
[97: SD498878]

Soil Light alkaline

Terrain Undulating

Altitude 61m/200ft

Area 6.5 hectares/16 acres

Gardeners 2 full-time

♿ Partially accessible

🐕 Guide dogs allowed

Other gardens in the area
Acorn Bank
Hill Top
Stagshaw
Holker Hall (not NT)
Levens Hall (not NT)

The Castle is surrounded by handsome grounds and a park with specimen trees and woodland walks. The garden is diverse with formal terraces, herbaceous borders, wall plants and roses, exceptionally good wild-flower meadow, orchard, a Dutch garden and a large limestone rock garden. Streams and rocky pools display moisture-loving plants, including National Collections of four genera of hardy ferns. Elsewhere in the garden grow shrubs and climbers, some tender on a south-facing wall. In the south garden species roses are underplanted with ground cover and bulbs.

Detail of the garden steps, with
Erigeron karvinskianus
(NTPL/Stephen Robson)

130

Snowshill Manor

Cottage garden designed by the Arts & Crafts architect, Charles Paget Wade, who gave Snowshill to the NT in 1951. Just as he filled the manor house with all manner of collections, so Wade decorated his garden with more collections – gate piers, troughs, cisterns and well heads. Walls and terraces form a series of small 'rooms', and a spring under the house has been used to create ponds and water spouts. Borders of herbs, shrubs and perennial plants, now cultivated on organic principles, provide great character and variety. The formal and informal areas, with planned light and shade, sustain the mystery and surprise. Wonderful views over the Cotswold landscape.

Apr	spring bulbs, blossom
May	perennials
Jun	roses, shrubs
Jul	roses, herbaceous, shrubs
Aug	herbaceous
Sep	herbaceous
Oct	autumn colour, berries
Win	closed

Snowshill, nr Broadway,
Gloucestershire WR12 7JU
Tel/Fax 01386 852410
Email
snowshillmanor@ntrust.org.uk

Location (1:L2) 2½ml SW of Broadway; turn from A44 Broadway bypass into Broadway village and by village green turn uphill to Snowshill [150: SP096339]

Soil Neutral loam

Terrain Hilly

Altitude 200m/656ft

Area 0.8 hectares/2 acres

Gardeners 2 full-time

Partially accessible

 Scented plants, guide dogs allowed

Plant sales Spring plant fair. Plant sales throughout the season

Events Guided tours of garden

Other gardens in the area
Hidcote Manor
Batsford Arboretum (not NT)
Bourton House (not NT)

View of Well garden from the cart shed (NTPL/Nick Meers)

Speke Hall

Apr	daffodills
May	rhododendrons
Jun	roses
Jul	roses
Aug	roses, borders
Sep	borders
Oct	
Win	snowdrops, crocus

The Walk, Liverpool, Liverpool
L24 1XD
Tel 0151 427 7231
Fax 0151 427 9860
Email spekehall@ntrust.org.uk

Location (7:H7) On N bank of
the Mersey, 1ml off A561 on W
side of Liverpool airport. Follow
airport signs from M62 exit 6,
A5300; M56 exit 12. Follow
brown signs [108: SJ419825]

Soil Acid, light soil

Terrain Flat terrain, exposed site
but mild climate

Altitude 30m/98ft

Area 7 hectares/17 acres

Gardeners 3 full-time

Great gardeners Graham Stuart
Thomas

Fully accessible

Braille guide, scented
plants, guide dogs allowed

Plant sales Annually in May

Events Walks with warden, re-
enactment weekends, Maize
Maze during summer holidays,
outdoor theatre in summer

Other gardens in the area
Dunham Massey
Croxteth Park (not NT)
Ness Garden (not NT)

The garden was redesigned between 1855 and 1865 for
Richard Watt. The present layout comprises of lawns,
borders, paths and hedges together with a dry moat.
A rose garden, laid out in 1984 and planted with shrub,
dwarf and clustered floribunda roses, is a fine feature on
the south side of the half-timbered hall. Stream garden
and extensive spring bulb planting. Rhododendrons
and bluebell woods with many woodland walks and
fine views over the Mersey Basin towards North Wales.
Three Victorian island beds have recently been
reinstated on the South Lawn.

Detail from the 17th-century bridge leading from the garden to the
north front (NTPL/Rupert Truman)

132

Springhill

A small estate in green rolling countryside with walks through woodland. Formal cottage gardens, mostly walled, including herb and herbaceous gardens, as well as shrubberies and copses and some fine ancient trees. The garden has a tranquil and serene character, perfectly complementing the 17th-century house and estate.

Apr	rhododendrons, bulbs
May	bluebells
Jun	herbaceous borders, roses
Jul	herbaceous borders, roses
Aug	herbaceous borders
Sep	autumn colour
Oct	autumn colour
Win	closed

Soil Light acid

Terrain Undulating, top of hill, rocky

Altitude 30m/98ft

Area 35 hectares/86 acres

Gardeners 1 full-time

Partially accessible

Scented plants, guide dogs allowed

dogs allowed on leads, in grounds only

Plant sales Annual plant sale in spring

20 Springhill Road, Moneymore, Magherafelt, Londonderry
BT45 7NQ
Tel/Fax 028 8674 8210
Email springhill@ntrust.org.uk

Location (1:G5) 1ml from Moneymore on Moneymore–Coagh road, B18 [H866828]

Sundial in one of the walled gardens (NTPL/Christopher Gallagher)

Stagshaw

Apr	spring bulbs and early rhododendrons
May	rhododendrons and azaleas
Jun	rhododendrons and azaleas
Jul	
Aug	closed
Sep	closed
Oct	closed
Win	closed

A woodland garden, created by the late Cubby Acland, Lake District regional agent for the NT. It contains a fine collection of trees and shrubs, including many notable rhododendrons, azaleas and camellias. The Skelghyll Woods, adjacent to the garden, offer delightful walks.

Ambleside, Cumbria LA22 0HE
Tel/Fax 015394 46027
Email stagshaw@ntrust.org.uk

Location (7:C6) ½ml S of
Ambleside on A591
[90: NY380029]

Soil Acid

Terrain Hillside

Altitude 70m/230ft

Area 3.2 hectares/8 acres

Gardeners 1 part-time

Not suitable for wheelchairs

Events NGS days twice a year

Other gardens in the area
Sizergh Castle
Broakhole (National Park) (not NT)
Holehead (not NT)

Rhododendrons and azaleas in the woodland garden
(NTPL/Stephen Robson)

Standen

Family house designed in the 1890s for the Beale family by the Arts & Crafts architect, Philip Webb. The gardens are the result of the ideas and vision of Margaret Beale, echoing the informal beauty of the William Morris wallpapers that decorate the house. They are set on several levels, with magnificent views over the valley, enabling visitors to stroll through the Bamboo garden, Rose garden, Rhododendron dell, and the Quarry garden with its newly restored bridge. The woodland walk, through nearby Hollybush wood, is a haven for bluebells and other wild flowers.

Apr	camellias, spring bulbs
May	scented azaleas and rhododendrons, cowslips
Jun	roses
Jul	irises
Aug	
Sep	
Oct	acers
Win	closed

East Grinstead, Sussex
RH19 4NE
Tel 01342 323029
Fax 01342 316424
Email standen@ntrust.org.uk

Location (2:G7) 2ml S of East Grinstead, signposted from B2110 (Turners Hill road) [187: TQ389356]

Soil Sandstone base and clay

Terrain Hillside

Altitude 60m/197ft

Area 4.85 hectares/12 acres

Gardeners 1 full-time, 1 part-time

Great gardeners William Robinson

 Partially accessible

Braille guide, scented plants, guide dogs allowed

Events Guided walks by arrangement

Other gardens in the area
Nymans
Sheffield Park
Borde Hill (not NT)
Leonardslee (not NT)

View from the house, with the Tulip tree (NT/David Sellman)

Stoneacre

Apr	spring flowers
May	spring flowers
Jun	herbaceous borders, roses
Jul	herbaceous borders, roses
Aug	herbaceous borders
Sep	
Oct	
Win	closed

A yeoman's house dating from the late 15th century, surrounded by a recently restored romantic garden with a large collection of unusual plants. The garden in front of the house consists of three lawns bounded by herbaceous borders and is enclosed by ragstone walls. A wild garden behind the house features fruit trees from the former orchard and a wetland area with a pond.

Otham, Maidstone, Kent
ME15 8RS
Tel 01622 862871
Fax 01622 862157

Location (2:J6) At N end of Otham village, 3ml SE of Maidstone, 1m S of A20 [188: TQ800535]

P

Soil Cretaceous lower greensand

Terrain Moderately steep-sided valley

Altitude 70m/230ft

Area 0.6 hectares/1 acre

Gardeners 1 part-time

Not suitable for wheelchairs

Scented plants, guide dogs allowed

Other gardens in the area
Scotney Castle
Sissinghurst Castle

Detail of the garden in front of the house (NTPL/Stephen Robson)

Stourhead

Magnificent landscape garden created by the wealthy banker, Sir Henry Hoare II, from 1741–80 as a reaction against the formal gardens of the 17th century. 'Natural' landscape dotted with classical temples surrounds a large artificial lake and presents an English 18th-century view of an Arcadian paradise. Eye-catchers include a Pantheon (containing a superb collection of sculpture from Henry Hoare's Grand Tour), Temple of Apollo, Temple of Flora and grottoes inhabited by a nymph and a river god. Richard Colt Hoare, grandson of Henry, added some unusual trees and shrubs but left his grandfather's basic scheme unaltered. Successive members of the family continued to develop the garden with exotic trees and shrubs: daffodils and magnolias in spring, and a stunning display of rhododendrons in early summer. Blazing autumn colour is provided by an extensive tree collection, including maples, Tulip trees and redwood. Pelargonium house in walled garden.

John Cheere's statue of a river god in his grotto (NTPL/Derek Croucher)

Apr	daffodils
May	magnolias, rhododendrons
Jun	rhododendrons
Jul	viburnum, magnolia, philadelphus
Aug	hydrangeas
Sep	hydrangeas, Indian bean tree
Oct	autumn colour
Win	

The Estate Office, Stourton, Warminster, Wiltshire BA12 6QD
Tel 01747 841152
Fax 01747 842005
Email stourhead@ntrust.org.uk

Location (1:K5) At Stourton, off B3092, 3ml NW of Mere (A303), 8ml S of Frome (A361). Parking 400m from house and garden adjacent to catering facilities. [183: ST778340]

Soil Acid greensand

Terrain Rolling hills

Altitude 155m/509ft

Area 38 hectares/94 acres

Gardeners 6 full-time, 1 part-time, 1/2 seasonal

Partially accessible

Braille guide, scented plants, guide dogs allowed

Plant sales Yes

Events Garden walks, talks, children's events, musical events

Other gardens in the area
Barrington Court
The Courts
Lacock Abbey
Montacute House
Prior Park
Tintinhull
East Lambrook Manor (not NT)
Hadspen House (not NT)

Stowe Landscape Gardens

Apr	interest all season
May	interest all season
Jun	interest all season
Jul	interest all season
Aug	interest all season
Sep	interest all season
Oct	interest all season
Win	interest all season

Buckingham, Buckinghamshire
MK18 5EH
Tel 01280 822850
Fax 01280 822437
Email
stowegarden@ntrust.org.uk

Location (2:D2) 3ml NW of
Buckingham via Stowe Avenue,
off A422 Buckingham–Banbury
road [152: SP665366]

The Palladian Bridge, the Gothic
Temple and the Cobham
Monument
(NTPL/Andrew Butler)

Regarded as the birthplace of the 18th-century
landscape garden in Britain. Throughout the century
the Temple family employed many leading architects,
gardeners and sculptors of the day, including Vanbrugh,
Bridgeman, Kent and Brown, to create an idealised
classical landscape. Decorated with temples, columns
and arches, different areas of the gardens such as the
Elysian Fields and Grecian Valley, through their
buildings, statuary and planting, evoke the classical
world so admired by the Georgians. Initially formal,
Stowe pioneered the movement towards more
naturalistic landscape of grassy vistas and informal
planting perpetuated by Capability Brown, head
gardener at Stowe from 1741.

Soil Lime-free, gravel and clay

Terrain Undulating

Altitude 90m/295ft

Area 142 hectares/351 acres

Gardeners 5 full-time

Great gardeners Capability
Brown, William Kent, Sir John
Vanbrugh, Charles Bridgeman

Not suitable for wheelchairs

Braille guide, scented
plants, guide dogs allowed

dogs allowed on leads

Events Please contact property
for full details

Other gardens in the area
Claydon House
Waddesdon Manor

Studley Royal Water Garden

Superb 18th-century landscaped water garden created by John Aislabie. Now the least-altered Georgian 'green' garden in England, with elegant ornamental lakes, avenues, temples and cascades providing a succession of unforgettable vistas in an atmosphere of peace and tranquillity. The landscape incorporates the spectacular remains of 12th-century Fountains Abbey, the Elizabethan Fountains Hall and a medieval deer park covering a further 120ha, where William Burges' 19th-century St Mary's Church provides a dramatic focal point. Made a World Heritage Site in 1986.

Apr	primroses
May	cowslips
Jun	oxlips
Jul	orchids
Aug	pinks
Sep	scabious
Oct	autumn colours
Win	snowdrops

Fountains, Ripon, Yorkshire
HG4 3DY
Tel 01765 608888 (Visitor Centre)
Fax 01765 601002 (Visitor Centre)

Location (8:C6) 4ml W of Ripon off B6265 to Pateley Bridge, signposted from the A1, 10ml N of Harrogate (A61)
[99: SE271683]

Soil Magnesian limestone and sandstone

Terrain Lowland

Altitude 100m/328ft

Area 60 hectares/148 acres

Gardeners 9 full-time

Partially accessible

Braille guide, scented plants, guide dogs allowed

dogs allowed on leads

Other gardens in the area
Beningbrough Hall
Newby Hall (not NT)

The Temple of Piety reflected in a moon pond
(NTPL/Geoff Morgan)

139

Sunnycroft

Apr	arum lilies
May	arum lilies
Jun	rhododendrons
Jul	herbaceous borders
Aug	cut flowers
Sep	herbaceous borders
Oct	
Win	closed

A late-Victorian gentleman's villa, typical of houses that were built at that time for prosperous business and professional people on the fringes of towns and cities. Sunnycroft is one of the few to have survived largely unaltered. Features of the garden include a Wellingtonia avenue, kitchen garden, a meadow, greenhouse, conservatory, peach house, orchard, shrubbery, herbaceous borders and cut-flower beds. Also croquet lawn, pigsties and stables.

200 Holyhead Road, Wellington,
Telford, Shropshire TF1 2DR
Tel 01743 708100

Location (6:C6) Exit M54 jct 7,
follow B5061 towards Wellington
[127: SJ652109]

Soil Sandy and silty loam

Terrain Flat

Altitude 113m/371ft

Area 2 hectares/5 acres

Gardeners 1 full-time

♿ Fully accessible

♿ Scented plants, guide dogs
allowed

Other gardens in the area
Attingham Park
Benthall Hall

The Edwardian terrace
(NTPL/Clive Boursnell)

Tatton Park

Set in rolling parkland, the formal gardens are full of delightful surprises and are considered to be amongst the most important in England. Attractions include the famous Japanese Garden which underwent large-scale restoration during 2001 with funding from the Japanese Exposition Fund and the NT. Extensive research by Professor Fukuhara of Osaka University and the existence of glass-plate photographic records have enabled the garden to be restored to its original 1910 design. The restoration of the Walled Garden began in December 2000, a project that will provide a number of new facilities as well as restoring fig, tomato, orchid and pot-plant houses.

Apr	rhododendrons, azaleas
May	rhododendrons, azaleas
Jun	shrub borders
Jul	shrub borders
Aug	herbaceous
Sep	herbaceous
Oct	autumn colour
Win	

Knutsford, Cheshire WA16 6QN
Tel 01625 534400
Fax 01625 534403
Email tatton@cheshire.gov.uk

Location (7:K7) 3½ml N of Knutsford, 4ml S of Altrincham, 5ml from M6, exit 19; 3ml from M56, exit 7, well signposted on A556; entrance on Ashley Road, 1½ml NE of jn. A5034 with A50 [109/118: SJ745815]

Soil Sandy

Terrain Flat

Altitude 60m/197ft

Area 20 hectares/49 acres

Gardeners 13 full-time

Great gardeners Graham Stuart Thomas

Partially accessible

Braille guide, scented plants, guide dogs allowed

Plant sales Plant Hunters' Fair

Events Guided tours of Japanese Garden

Other gardens in the area
Apprentice House Garden,
  Quarry Bank Mill
Dunham Massey
Little Moreton Hall
Arley Hall (not NT)

The Japanese Garden (NTPL/Clive Boursnell)

Tintinhull House

Apr	tulips, wallflowers, magnolias
May	foliage
Jun	mixed herbaceous borders
Jul	roses, herbaceous borders
Aug	mixed herbaceous borders
Sep	dahlias, asters
Oct	closed
Win	closed

Farm St, Tintinhull, Yeovil,
Somerset BA22 9PZ
Tel 01935 822545
Email tintinhull@ntrust.org.uk

Location (1:J6) 5ml NW of
Yeovil, ½ml S of A303, on E
outskirts of Tintinhull
[183: ST503198]

Soil Neutral

Terrain Level

Altitude 30m/98ft

Area 0.8 hectares/2 acres

Gardeners 2 full-time

Great gardeners Phyllis Reiss,
Penelope Hobhouse

 Partially accessible

 Scented plants, guide dogs
allowed

Plant sales Occasional

Other gardens in the area
Barrington Court
Lytes Cary
Montacute House
East Lambrook Manor (not NT)
Hadspen House (not NT)

View from the kitchen garden
into the pool garden
(NTPL/Nick Meers)

Tintinhull House Garden is a tiny, delightful walled
garden divided into separate areas by clipped hedges.
Largely the inspiration of Mrs Phyllis Reiss who
moved to Tintinhull in 1933. Domes of box line the
central path leading from the west front of the 17th-
century house (not open) to the different 'rooms',
including an azalea garden, a fountain garden planted
with white-flowering and silver plants around a central
pool, and a kitchen garden with espaliered fruit trees
and paths edged with catmint. The more formal flower
garden features a rectangular pool flanked with long
beds carefully planned for flower and foliage effects.
The east-facing bed contains a vivid colour scheme of
yellows, oranges and scarlet, while the opposite bed
features contrasting pastel colours.

Trelissick

Beautifully situated at the head of the Fal Estuary above the King Harry Ferry, the estate commands panoramic views over the area and has extensive park and woodland walks beside the River Fal. At the heart is the tranquil garden, set on many levels and containing a superb collection of tender and exotic plants which give colour throughout the year. The display of spring-flowering plants and shrubs is particularly spectacular. Drifts of daffodils and narcissus in spring are followed by wild flowers in summer. Features include a wildlife pond, several thatched summer-houses and a traditional Cornish apple orchard containing many original varieties, some nearly extinct. The house is not open but there is an art and craft gallery, and a fine Georgian stable block. There is also a Celtic cross and a sensory garden for visually-impaired visitors. Holds the National Collections of Photinia and Azara.

Soil Acid, clay loam

Terrain Promontory with steep slopes to estuary shores

Altitude 30m/98ft

Area 10 hectares/25 acres

Gardeners 4 full-time, 1 seasonal

Great gardeners Graham Stuart Thomas, John Sales

Partially accessible

Braille guide, scented plants, guide dogs allowed

dogs allowed

Plant sales Regular plant sales

Events Guided walks, drama in summer

Other gardens in the area
Glendurgan
Trewithen (not NT)
Caerhays (not NT)
The Eden Project (not NT)
The Lost Gardens of Heligan (not NT)
Lamorran House (not NT)
Trebah (not NT)

Apr	rhododendrons, camellias, bulbs
May	rhododendrons, wistaria
Jun	herbaceous
Jul	hydrangeas, wild flowers
Aug	hydrangeas, herbaceous beds
Sep	herbaceous beds
Oct	autumn colour
Win	camellias, rhododendrons, azaleas, bulbs

Feock, nr Truro, Cornwall
TR3 6QL
Tel 01872 862090
Fax 01872 865808
Email trelissick@ntrust.org.uk

Location (1:C9) 4ml S of Truro, on both sides of B3289 above King Harry Ferry
[204: SW837396]

Ferris's Cottage in the Dell (NTPL/Stephen Robson)

143

Trengwainton

Apr	rhododendrons, bluebells
May	rhododendrons, stream garden
Jun	stream garden
Jul	watsonias, altonias and summer bulbs
Aug	agapanthus, herbaceous beds
Sep	hydrangeas
Oct	autumn colour
Win	magnolias, camellias, rhododendron, spring flowers

nr Penzance, Cornwall
TR20 8RZ
Tel 01736 362297 (opening hours only)
Fax 01736 362297
Email trengwainton@ntrust.org.uk

Location (1:B9) 2ml NW of Penzance, ½ml W of Heamoor off Penzance–Morvah road (B3312), ½ml off St Just road (A3071) [203: SW445315]

Trengwainton, which in Cornish means 'house of spring', is a plantsman's paradise. The favourable climate allows many rare plants to be grown unprotected against frost. The unusual walled garden, constructed in 1820 for early vegetable crops, now houses a wonderful collection of trees and shrubs planted by the Bolitho family during the 20th century. Some rhododendrons flowered at Trengwainton for the first time in the UK after being collected by Frank Kingdon-Ward. As well as its stunning collections of rhododendrons, camellias and magnolias, the garden has a stream running almost its entire length, with plantings of astilbe, primula and New Zealand tree ferns. The garden's spring flowers start very early owing to its location. Some special large trees include *Rhododendron* 'Morvah', *Cornus Capitata* 'Madon'. There are also numerous rare shrubs. A walk to the top of the garden gives magnificent views over Mount's Bay.

Soil Acid loam on granite

Terrain Gentle incline

Altitude 100m/328ft

Area 50 hectares/124 acres

Gardeners 4 full-time

Great gardeners Frank Kingdon-Ward

Partially accessible

Scented plants, guide dogs allowed

dogs allowed

Plant sales Regular plant sales

Other gardens in the area
Glendurgan
St Michael's Mount
Trelissick
Tresco Abbey (not NT)
Trevarno (not NT)

Primula heladoxa in the stream garden (NTPL/Nick Meers)

Trerice

Small summer garden with enclosed courts, lawns and bowling green. The garden surrounds an Elizabethan manor house, but there are no surviving garden features from that period. The orchard and fruit trees, including some Cornish varieties, are planted in 17th-century quincunx pattern. Collection of perennials, climbers and shrubs: back court with fuchsias, lonicera and roses; front walled courtyard with herbaceous borders on a purple/gold theme devised by Graham Stuart Thomas. The small kitchen garden supplies organic produce for the restaurant's Elizabethan 'salats'. The Hayloft houses a collection representing the history of the lawnmower.

Apr	spring bulbs
May	apple blossom
Jun	wistaria
Jul	roses, vine
Aug	early apples
Sep	apple main crop
Oct	autumn colour
Win	closed

Kestle Mill, nr Newquay, Cornwall
TR8 4PG
Tel 01637 875404
Fax 01637 879300
Email trerice@ntrust.org.uk

Location (1:C8) 3ml SE of Newquay via A392 and A3058 (turn right at Kestle Mill) [200: SW841585]

Soil Neutral

Terrain Terraced

Altitude 30m/98ft

Area 5.7 hectares/14 acres

Gardeners 1 full-time

Great gardeners Graham Stuart Thomas

♿ Partially accessible

Plant sales Ongoing through season

Events Apple Week, October

Other gardens in the area
Lanhydrock
Chyverton (not NT)
The Eden Project (not NT)
Probus Demonstration Garden (not NT)
Trehane (not NT)
Trewithen (not NT)

Two examples from the lawnmower collection, in front of the house (NT/Andrew Besley)

145

Upton House

Apr	narcissus, spring bedding
May	spring flowers, cherry trees
Jun	herbaceous borders, bog planting
Jul	herbaceous borders, roses
Aug	vegetable garden
Sep	asters, autumn foliage
Oct	asters
Win	closed

Banbury, Warwickshire
OX15 6HT
Tel 01295 670266
Email uptonhouse@ntrust.org.uk

Location (6:F9) On A422, 7ml
NW of Banbury, 12ml SE of
Stratford-upon-Avon
[151: SP371461]

Soil Alkaline, light

Terrain Valley site with terraces.
Moderately exposed, part frost
pocket

Altitude 213m/699ft

Area 15 hectares/37 acres

Gardeners 5 full-time

Great gardeners Kitty Lloyd-
Jones

 Partially accessible

 Braille guide, scented
plants, guide dogs allowed

Events Guided walks

Other gardens in the area
Canons Ashby
Charlecote Park
Farnborough Hall
Hidcote Manor
Broughton Castle (not NT)

An extensively planted garden created by the 2nd
Lord Bearsted after 1927, overlaying late 17th-century
features. The main garden lies hidden beyond the lawn
south of the house and is reached by a grand, 20th-
century stone staircase by Percy Morley Horder, the
architect who remodelled the house. This leads to a
series of terraces housing the National Collection of
Asters with a kitchen garden below, still used for
growing fruit and vegetables. This is bounded to the
south by a lake, to the east by double herbaceous
borders and to the west by two small formal gardens,
one a yew-enclosed rose garden, the other for assorted
flowers. Cascades of wistaria and spray roses overhang
the terrace. The beds along the south front of the
house are planted in blue and yellow. Below the house
to the west is a yew walk and bog garden with what
was once a banqueting pavilion. Miss Kitty Lloyd-
Jones advised Lady Bearsted on the planting of the
ornamental area of the slope.

The aster border (NTPL/Stephen Robson)

The Vyne

The grounds of the house built in the early 16th century by Lord Sandys, Henry VIII's Lord Chamberlain. A variety of annual and perennial flowerbeds and spectacular herbaceous borders including the Summer-house Garden which has been transformed into an Edwardian-style flower garden with beds designed to reflect the architectural floor plan of the summer-house – one of the oldest garden buildings in the country, c.1632-36. The orchard and Edwardian Wild Garden provide a delightfully informal contrast, and there are also attractive lakeside and woodland walks. Good collection of ancient trees, including the 'Hundred Guinea Oak' believed to be around 650 years old.

Apr	spring bedding display
May	bluebells
Jun	roses
Jul	herbaceous beds
Aug	herbaceous beds
Sep	early apples, plums
Oct	apples, plums, liquidambar, parrotia
Win	bulbs, spring flowers, witch hazel

Sherborne St John, Basingstoke, Hampshire RG24 9HL
Tel 01256 883858
Fax 01256 881720
Email thevyne@ntrust.org.uk

Location (2:D6) 4ml N of Basingstoke between Bramley and Sherborne St John.
[175 & 186: SU637566]

Soil Clay

Terrain Undulating

Altitude 60m/197ft

Area 5 hectares/12 acres

Gardeners 2 full-time, 1 part-time

 Partially accessible

Scented plants, guide dogs allowed

Plant sales Spring Plant Fair, May

Events For details call 01256 883858

Other gardens in the area
Basildon Park
Hinton Ampner
Mottisfont Abbey
West Green House
Englefield House (not NT)
Savill Garden (not NT)
Welford Park (not NT)

One of the herbaceous borders (NTPL/Andrea Jones)

Waddesdon Manor

Apr	spring bedding, tulips
May	spring bedding, tulips
Jun	roses, summer bedding
Jul	roses, summer bedding
Aug	summer bedding
Sep	autumn bedding
Oct	
Win	closed Jan and Feb

Waddesdon, nr Aylesbury,
Buckinghamshire HP18 0JH
Tel 01296 653203
Fax 01296 653212
Email
waddesdonmanor@ntrust.org.uk

Location (2:D3) Access via
Waddesdon village, 6ml NW of
Aylesbury on A41; M40
(westbound) exit 6 or 7 via
Thame & Long Crendon or M40
(eastbound) exit 9 via Bicester
[165: SP740169]

French Renaissance-style chateau set in parkland
and formal gardens, created by Baron Ferdinand
de Rothschild in the 1880s from a bare hilltop site
and bequeathed to the NT in 1957 by the late James
de Rothschild. One of the most impressive high-
Victorian gardens in Britain, famous for its landscape
of specimen trees, formal parterres and striking
seasonal displays. Outstanding collection of sculpture
and two ornamental fountains. Splendid collection of
exotic birds in rococo-style aviary of filigree cast iron.

Soil Clay

Terrain Exposed hilltop site

Altitude 75m/246ft

Area 67 hectares/166 acres

Gardeners 11 full-time

Partially accessible

Guide dogs allowed

Events Please contact property
for full details

Other gardens in the area
Claydon House
Stowe Landscape Gardens

The South Fountain in the parterre
(NT Waddeson Manor/Hugh Palmer)

Wakehurst Place

A vibrant, constantly developing garden, often described as one of the most beautiful in England, managed by the Royal Botanic Gardens, Kew. A series of ornamental features with many plants from across the world provide year-round colour and interest. Extensive woodlands, including an informal arboretum and secluded valley, offer delightful walks. The ornamental gardens are set around an Elizabethan mansion. The Loder Valley Nature Reserve may also be visited by permit (24 hours' notice required).

Note: The Millennium Seed Bank, adjacent to Wakehurst Place, aims to house seeds from 10 per cent of the world's flora by 2009, to save species from extinction in the wild. The interactive exhibition in the Orange Room follows the journey of a seed from identification and collection, through to drying and cold storage in massive underground vaults. Entry free for NT members, and included in gardens entry fee.

Apr	magnolias, pieris, rhododendrons
May	bluebells, Chilean fire bush
Jun	giant Himalayan lilies, blue poppies, irises
Jul	irises, walled gardens, mixed borders
Aug	mixed borders, summer bedding
Sep	mixed borders, summer bedding
Oct	autumn colour
Win	winter garden, spring plantings

Ardingly, nr Haywards Heath, Sussex RH17 6TN
Tel 01444 894066
Fax 01444 894069
Email wakehurst@kew.org

Location (2:G7) 1½ml NW of Ardingly, on B2028
[187: TQ339314]

Soil Clay

Terrain Undulating

Altitude 150m/492ft

Area 227 hectares/561 acres

Gardeners Under administration of Royal Botanic Gardens, Kew full-time

Great gardeners Gerald Loder

 Partially accessible

Scented plants, guide dogs allowed

Plant sales March to October

Events Guided walks, Tuesdays, Thursdays, weekends and bank holidays throughout the year, Tours of the Loder Valley Reserve bank holidays and weekends from April to October

Other gardens in the area
Nymans
Sheffield Park
Standen

Rhododendrons in the woods
(NTPL/Michael C. Brown)

Wallington

Apr	bulbs, woodland flora
May	blossom, tulips
Jun	mixed borders
Jul	bedding, mixed borders
Aug	dahlias, mixed borders
Sep	anemones, asters
Oct	autumn colour
Win	conservatory, winter garden

Cambo, Morpeth,
Northumberland NE61 4AR
Tel 01670 774283
Fax 01670 774420
Email wallington@ntrust.org.uk

Location (9:J6) 12ml W of
Morpeth (B6343), 6ml NW of
Belsay (A696), take B6342 to
Cambo [81: NZ030843]

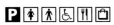

Soil Clay loam/medium loam

Terrain Undulating

Altitude 152m/499ft

Area 26 hectares/64 acres

Gardeners 5 full-time,
1 seasonal

Great gardeners Capability
Brown, Graham Stuart Thomas

[&] Partially accessible

[&] Scented plants, guide dogs
allowed

[&] dogs allowed on leads

Events Guided walks, gardening
demonstration day, family fun
day, concerts

Other gardens in the area
Washington Old Hall
Alnwick Castle (not NT)
Belsay (not NT)
Chillingham Castle (not NT)
Herterton (not NT)
Hexham Herbs (not NT)
Howick Hall (not NT)

The style of the gardens and parkland are derived from the scheme of the 18th century, when Sir Walter Blackett established the balance of woodland, open meadow and ponds, together with much of the sculpture and buildings. The mature trees give the garden a sense of history and harmony.

The walled garden, created in 1760 as a vegetable garden, now shelters Wallington's most delicate plants, with a conservatory restored in 1988.

An urn in the ornamental walled garden (NTPL/Andrea Jones)

Washington Old Hall

The modest 17th-century manor house was the ancestral home of George Washington, first President of the United States. The garden is small and newly created, filled with English flowers and herbs of the 17th century, some of which are now rare. The parterre is also in formal Jacobean style. Other features include a walled border with buttresses, beech 'elbow' hedging, a formal pathed lawn with a wildflower mead and formal hedging.

Apr	
May	tulips
Jun	herbs
Jul	herbs
Aug	espaliered fruit
Sep	
Oct	
Win	closed

Soil Loam and clay

Terrain Level

Altitude 65m/213ft

Area hectares/ acres

Gardeners 2 part-time

 Partially accessible

 Braille guide, scented plants, guide dogs allowed

on lead only

Events 4th July Independence celebration

Other gardens in the area
Cragside
Wallington
Belsay (not NT)

The meadow garden
(NTPL/Nick Meers)

The Avenue, District 4,
Washington Village, Tyne & Wear
NE38 7LE
Tel 0191 416 6879
Fax 0191 419 2065

Location (9:K7) 5ml W of Sunderland, 2ml E of A1, S of Tyne tunnel, follow signs to Washington, District 4, then Washington village; situated on E side of Avenue (adj. to church) Signposted from A1231
[88: NZ312566]

The Weir

Apr	wild flowers
May	bluebells
Jun	tway-blades
Jul	hypericum
Aug	cyclamen
Sep	
Oct	autumn colour
Win	snowdrops, spring bulbs

Swainshill, nr Hereford, HR4 8BS
Tel 01981 590509
Email theweir@ntrust.org.uk

Location (6:B9) 5ml W of
Hereford on A438
[149: SO435421]

One of the first NT gardens to open in spring.
A largely informal garden, with riverside walk and
views across the River Wye and the Herefordshire
countryside to the Black Mountains and Hay Bluff.
Providing a diverse range of habitats, the garden is rich
in wildlife including birds, butterflies, damselflies and
dragonflies. Banks of primroses and violets provide a
perfect foil for naturalised snowdrops, narcissus and
chionodoxa, giving way to *Scilla italica*. These are
followed by bluebells scattered through the unimproved
grasslands which contain a variety of native plants
including tway-blades and quaking grass. River bank
shows Roman masonry *in situ*, probably a quay or even
bridge abutments.

Soil Light loam/silt alkaline

Terrain Steep banks on flood
plain, river valley

Altitude 61m/200ft

Area 4 hectares/10 acres

Gardeners 2 full-time

 Partially accessible

Guide dogs allowed

Events Wildlife fair (June), guided
walks by arrangement, bat walks
on summer evenings, wildlife
training days

Other gardens in the area
Berrington Hall
Brockhampton Estate
Croft Castle
Burford Gardens (not NT)
Hergest Croft (not NT)
Hampton Court, Herefordshire
(not NT)

Early spring bulbs (NTPL/Stephen Robson)

West Green House

The original garden at West Green House hides behind walls dating from the mid-1770s which form individual compartments, the largest still essentially true to its 18th-century design. Each garden within the garden creates a different atmosphere, each with a highly descriptive name: the Green Theatre, the Nymphaeum, the Lake Field, the Alice in Wonderland garden, the Snowdrop Lawn. Formality is tempered by quirky topiaries, subtle plantings and the hint of a wilderness garden spied from the gates in the walls.

Apr	daffodils, tulips
May	peonies
Jun	roses
Jul	penstemon, campanula
Aug	dahlias, asters
Sep	
Oct	
Win	snowdrops, daffodils

West Green, Hartley Wintney, Hampshire RG27 8JB
Tel/Fax 01252 844611

Location (2:D6) 1ml W of Hartley Wintney, 10ml NE of Basingstoke, 1ml N of A30 [175: SU745564]

Soil Heavy clay

Terrain Level

Altitude 68.5m/225ft

Area 3 hectares/7 acres

Gardeners 2 full-time, 1 part-time

Partially accessible

Scented plants, guide dogs allowed

Plant sales Phone for details

Events Phone for details

Other gardens in the area
The Vyne

Ornamental cabbage in the kitchen garden
(NTPL/Andrea Jones)

West Wycombe Park

Apr	interest all season
May	interest all season
Jun	interest all season
Jul	interest all season
Aug	interest all season
Sep	interest all season
Oct	interest all season
Win	interest all season

A rococo landscape garden largely created by the 2nd Sir Francis Dashwood in the 1730s, inspired by his Grand Tours on the Continent. The house and garden are sited in a valley with a dammed river forming a lake and cascade. The garden contains a series of classical temples and follies, some of which were designed by Nicholas Revett, including a cottage disguised as a church. Fine trees.

West Wycombe,
Buckinghamshire HP14 3AJ
Tel 01494 513569

Location (2:E4) At W end of
West Wycombe, S of the Oxford
road (A40) [175: SU828947]

Soil Limy

Terrain Valley site

Altitude 75m/246ft

Area 18.6 hectares/46 acres

Gardeners 1 full-time, 1 part-time

♿ Partially accessible

Other gardens in the area
Cliveden
Hughenden Manor
Stowe Landscape Gardens
Waddesdon Manor

The 18th-century house in its landscape (NTPL/Andrew Butler)

Westbury Court

A walled Dutch-style water garden originally laid out by local gentleman, Maynard Colchester, and his nephew between 1696 and 1714. Restored from dereliction by the Trust from 1967, using detailed accounts and contemporary bird's-eye view by Johannes Kipp. The majority of plants now grown were available to the original owner. Good collection of espaliered apples and pears with 17th-century species chosen such as 'Catshead' and 'Bellisime d'Hiver'. Four-hundred-year-old Holm oak and reputedly the tallest Tulip tree (*Liriodendron tulipifera*) in Britain. Formal parterre with topiary and historical planting gives good displays in summer. Walled flower garden provides colour all summer long. Picnic area planted with daffodils, snowdrops and wild flowers, providing a haven for wildlife.

Apr	spring bulbs
May	blossom
Jun	walled garden
Jul	parterre, topiary, waterlilies
Aug	parterre, fruit
Sep	fruit
Oct	autumn colour
Win	closed

Westbury-on-Severn,
Gloucestershire GL14 1PD
Tel/Fax 01452 760461
Email
westburycourt@ntrust.org.uk

Location (1:K2) 9ml SW of
Gloucester on A48
[162: SO718138]

Espaliered, 17th-century species of apples (NTPL/Ian Shaw)

Soil Silty loam, alkaline, medium
soil

Terrain Flat, susceptible to
flooding

Altitude 9m/30ft

Area 2 hectares/5 acres

Gardeners 1 full-time

Fully accessible

Braille guide, scented
plants, guide dogs allowed

Plant sales Spring plant fair

Events Summer musical
concert, Apple Day

Other gardens in the area
The Weir
How Caple Court (not NT)
Lydney Park (not NT)
Misarden Park (not NT)
Painswick (not NT)

Wightwick Manor

Apr	bulbs
May	rhododendrons, early shrubs
Jun	herbaceous , roses
Jul	herbaceous borders, roses
Aug	herbaceous borders, roses
Sep	herbaceous borders, autumn colour
Oct	autumn colour
Win	early bulbs

Wightwick Bank,
Wolverhampton, West Midlands
WV6 8EE
Tel 01902 761108
Fax 01902 764663
Email
wightwickmanor@ntrust.org.uk

Location (6:C6) 3ml W of
Wolverhampton, up Wightwick
Bank (off A454 beside the
Mermaid Inn) [139: SO869985]

Soil Lime free on sandstone

Terrain South, south-west
sloping site

Altitude 75m/246ft

Area 7 hectares/17 acres

Gardeners 3 full-time,
1 part-time

Great gardeners Thomas
Mawson

 Partially accessible

 Guide dogs allowed

 dogs allowed

Events Guided tours, talks, slide
shows and exhibitions

Other gardens in the area
Hodnet Hall (not NT)
Weston Park (not NT)

An attractive Victorian/Edwardian garden containing formal beds, a pergola, yew hedges and herbaceous borders. A self-contained landscape in urban setting around late 19th-century house built by Theodore Mander, an admirer of William Morris. Alfred Parsons RA advised first, followed by Thomas Mawson whose plan of 1910 was largely implemented including the terrace with characteristic steps and balustrade. One terrace contains the Poets' Garden with plants from the gardens of Shelley and Keats. Yew Walk leads to shrubberies, paddocks, trees, streams and two large ponds. Also a replica of the Mathematical Bridge at Queens' College, Cambridge. Collection of pelargoniums.

Wistaria and azaleas (NTPL/Ian Shaw)

Wimpole Hall

The formal parterre to the north of the hall is laid out in Union Jack style, best in May for tulips and in July for geraniums. Excellent display of daffodils and narcissus in May.

The newly restored walled garden contains the rebuilt 1790s glasshouses by Sir John Soane. There is a full hectare of walled vegetable garden, the produce of which is used in the restaurant.

The pleasure ground section is mainly an arboretum with native and ornamental species, and a National Collection of Walnut Trees. The garden occasionally hosts sculpture exhibitions.

Apr	daffodils
May	parterre
Jun	vegetables, cut flowers
Jul	parterre
Aug	parterre
Sep	
Oct	autumn colour
Win	

Arrington, Royston,
Cambridgeshire SG8 0BW
Tel 01223 207257
Fax 01223 207838
Email wimpolehall@ntrust.org.uk

Location (4:E6) 8ml SW of Cambridge (A603), 6ml N of Royston (A1198)
[154: TL336510]

Soil Clay

Terrain Gentle rolling countryside

Altitude 30m/98ft

Area 30 hectares/74 acres

Gardeners 3 full-time, 1 seasonal

Great gardeners Capability Brown, William Emes, Charles Bridgeman, Humphry Repton

 Fully accessible

 Braille guide, scented plants, guide dogs allowed

Plant sales In stable block shop

Events Plant fair in May

Other gardens in the area
Anglesey Abbey
Peckover House
Cambridge Botanic Gardens (not NT)

The formal parterre (NTPL/Nick Meers)

157

Winkworth Arboretum

Apr	flowering trees, bluebells
May	flowering trees & shrubs
Jun	flowering shrubs, herbaceous borders
Jul	trees & shrubs, herbaceous borders
Aug	trees & shrubs
Sep	trees & shrubs
Oct	autumn colour
Win	snowdrops, rhododendrons, mahonia, witch hazel

A peaceful arboretum on a hillside setting with stunning views over the hills and two lakes with a delightful old boathouse. Spectacular spring and autumn colours from rare trees and shrubs laid out in group plantings. In April the slopes turn into blue mists of bluebells. One of the finest collections of Sorbus in the country. Walking along the paths that lead through the trees affords excellent views as the sun strikes through the autumn-tinted foliage or lights up the coloured fruits. Good use of Blue Atlas Cedar to enhance the spring and autumn colours. Interesting fungi in autumn.

Hascombe Road, Godalming,
Surrey GU8 4AD
Tel 01483 208477
Fax 01483 208252
Email
winkwortharboretum@ntrust.org.uk

Location (2:F7) Nr Hascombe, 2ml SE of Godalming on E side of B2130. Discount for cycle and public transport users.
[169/170/186: SU990412]

Other gardens in the area
Clandon Park
Claremont
Hatchlands Park
Polesden Lacey
Munstead Woods (not NT)
Painshiill Park (not NT)
RHS Wisley (not NT)

Spectacular autumn colours
(NTPL/John Miller)

Soil Acid greensand

Terrain Steep

Altitude 100m/328ft

Area 44 hectares/109 acres

Gardeners 3 full-time

Great gardeners Graham Stuart Thomas, Dr Wilfred Fox

  Partially accessible

  Scented plants, guide dogs allowed

  on leads only

Events Guided tours, lunch lectures, NGS open days

Wordsworth House

A blend of cottage-style planting within a Georgian town garden framework. The terrace at the bottom of the garden overlooks the River Derwent and was a favourite play area for William Wordsworth and his sister Dorothy. The walled vegetable garden contains a range of traditional vegetable varieties as well as soft fruit, herbs and apples. The walls of the garden are planted with apples and pears trained as espaliers as well as *Clematis montana* and various hybrids. The main borders contain many old favourites such as phlox, pinks, geraniums, poppies and monkshood. The front garden is planted in typical simple Georgian style.

Apr	
May	fruit trees, herbs, roses, kitchen garden
Jun	fruit trees, herbs, roses, sweet peas, kitchen garden
Jul	fruit trees, herbs, roses, sweet peas, kitchen garden
Aug	fruit, herbs
Sep	fruit
Oct	
Win	closed

Main Street, Cockermouth,
Cumbria CA13 9RX
Tel/Fax 01900 824805
Email
wordsworthhouse@ntrust.org.uk

Soil Rich alluvial

Terrain Flat

Altitude 50m/164ft

Area 0.2 hectares/0 acres

Gardeners 1 part-time

Partially accessible

Guide dogs allowed

Events Meet the gardener

Other gardens in the area
Acorn Bank
Hill Top
Stagshaw
Dalmain (not NT)
Mire House (not NT)
Muncaster Garden (not NT)

Location (7:B5) Parking in town centre car parks. Map of car parks available at main entrance and shop [89: NY118307]

The garden where William Wordsworth and his sister used to play when they were young (NTPL/Magnus Rew)

159

Special features

	Formal features	Topiary	Pre-Victorian landscape	Victorian/Edwardian features	Inter-war garden	Post-war garden	Rose garden/beds	Herb garden/borders	Fruit and vegetables	Rare trees and shrubs	Water garden	Rock garden	Herbaceous and mixed borders	Conservatory	Orangery	Grotto	Wild flower areas
Acorn Bank Garden							●	●		●			●				●
Alfriston Clergy House	●	●					●	●	●				●				●
Anglesey Abbey	●	●	●	●	●	●				●	●		●				●
Antony	●	●	●				●			●	●		●				●
Apprentice House Garden, Quarry Bank Mill				●				●	●								
Ardress							●	●	●				●				●
The Argory	●		●				●		●								●
Arlington Court	●		●						●	●	●	●	●				●
Ascott	●	●								●	●		●			●	
Attingham Park			●												●		●
Avebury Manor	●	●	●				●		●				●				
Baddesley Clinton	●	●	●	●			●	●	●		●		●				●
Barrington Court	●		●				●	●		●			●				
Bateman's	●		●	●			●	●	●				●				●
Belton House	●	●	●	●									●		●		●
Beningbrough Hall	●	●	●						●	●			●	●			●
Benthall Hall			●														
Berrington Hall	●		●	●	●	●	●	●	●				●				●
Biddulph Grange Garden	●	●		●						●	●	●					
Blickling Hall	●	●	●										●		●		
Bodnant	●			●						●	●		●	●			●
Buckland Abbey	●	●						●	●				●				●
Buscot Park	●	●	●	●		●	●				●	●	●				
Calke Abbey	●		●						●	●			●			●	●
Canons Ashby			●	●			●	●	●	●			●				●
Castle Drogo	●	●		●			●	●	●	●			●				●
Castle Ward	●		●	●						●	●	●					●
Charlecote Park	●	●	●	●									●				
Chartwell					●	●	●			●	●		●				
Chastleton	●	●	●														
Chirk Castle	●	●	●		●	●	●			●	●	●	●				●
Clandon Park	●	●	●				●						●			●	
Claremont	●	●														●	
Clevedon Court												●					
Cliveden	●	●	●	●		●				●	●		●	●		●	●
Clumber Park			●	●	●					●	●		●	●	●		
Colby Woodland Garden										●			●				

Of organic interest	Of historic interest	Working kitchen garden	Produce for sale	Working orchard	Full wheelchair access	Partial wheelchair access	Unsuitable for wheelchairs	Scented plants	Careership/student posts	National Collections
	●	●	●			●		●		
●	●					●				
					●			●	●	
					●			●	●	Hemerocallis, Camellia japonica
●	●	●	●	●		●				
			●			●				Old Irish varieties of apple trees
						●		●		Escallonia (Slinger Collection)
		●				●		●		
	●					●		●		
	●				●	●		●		
					●					
●	●		●	●	●			●	●	
	●	●	●	●	●			●	●	
					●	●		●		
						●			●	
●	●	●	●	●	●	●		●		
					●	●		●		
			●	●	●			●		Apples
						●			●	
						●			●	
						●		●	●	Embothrium, Magnolia, Eucryphia, Rhododendron forrestii
	●					●		●		
						●				
	●	●	●	●		●		●		
		●	●			●		●		
●					●			●		
						●		●	●	
					●					
						●		●		
●						●				
						●		●	●	
					●	●		●		
●						●				
						●		●		
						●		●	●	Catalpa species
●	●	●	●	●		●		●	●	
						●				

	Formal features	Topiary	Pre-Victorian landscape	Victorian/Edwardian features	Inter-war garden	Post-war garden	Rose garden/beds	Herb garden/borders	Fruit and vegetables	Rare trees and shrubs	Water garden	Rock garden	Herbaceous and mixed borders	Conservatory	Orangery	Grotto	Wild flower areas
Coleton Fishacre	●			●						●	●		●				●
Compton Castle							●										
Cotehele	●			●			●	●	●	●			●				●
The Courts	●	●	●	●	●	●	●	●	●		●	●	●	●		●	●
Cragside	●			●						●	●	●					●
Croome Park			●							●	●			●	●	●	
Dudmaston					●		●			●	●	●	●				
Dunham Massey	●		●	●						●	●		●		●		●
Dunster Castle					●	●				●			●	●	●		
Dyrham Park	●	●	●				●			●	●		●		●		●
East Riddlesden Hall									●				●				●
Emmetts Garden				●			●			●		●					●
Erddig	●			●			●	●	●				●				●
Farnborough Hall	●		●								●						
Felbrigg Hall	●		●				●	●	●				●		●		
Fenton House		●					●	●	●				●				
Florence Court	●		●	●			●			●							●
Gawthorpe Hall	●			●			●										●
Glendurgan				●						●			●				●
Greenway				●		●				●		●	●	●		●	●
Greys Court	●	●					●	●	●	●			●				
Gunby Hall	●	●	●	●			●	●	●	●		●	●	●			●
Ham House	●	●	●				●	●	●						●		●
Hanbury Hall	●	●	●	●						●	●		●		●		●
Hardwick Hall								●					●				●
Hardy's Cottage													●				
Hare Hill							●			●		●					
Hatchlands Park	●			●			●										●
Hidcote Manor	●	●		●			●			●			●				
Hill Top									●				●				
Hinton Ampner	●	●			●	●	●			●	●		●				●
Hughenden Manor	●			●						●			●				●
Ickworth	●	●	●				●			●			●	●	●		●
Ightham Mote								●	●		●		●				
Kedleston Hall		●													●		
Killerton	●		●	●						●		●	●				●
Kingston Lacy	●			●			●			●			●				●

Of organic interest	Of historic interest	Working kitchen garden	Produce for sale	Working orchard	Full wheelchair access	Partial wheelchair access	Unsuitable for wheelchairs	Scented plants	Careership/student posts	National Collections
						●		●	○	
						●		●		
			○			●			○	
						●		●	○	
						●				
				●		●				
					●			●		
●						●			○	
						●		●	○	Arbutus
						●			○	
●						●		●		
						●				
			○			●		●		Hedera
						●				
					●	●		●		Colchicum
	●					●		●		
					●			●		
						●		●		
							●		○	
						●		●		
●	●		●			●		●	○	
●	●	●				●			○	
	●		●	●		●				
						●		●	○	Scabiosa caucasica
						●		●		
						●		●		
				●						
						●		●		
	●	●				●		●		
					●			●		
●			●	●		●				
						●		●	○	Buxus
						●				
						●		●		
						●		●		
					●				○	Anemone nemorosa, Convallaria

	Formal features	Topiary	Pre-Victorian landscape	Victorian/Edwardian features	Inter-war garden	Post-war garden	Rose garden/beds	Herb garden/borders	Fruit and vegetables	Rare trees and shrubs	Water garden	Rock garden	Herbaceous and mixed borders	Conservatory	Orangery	Grotto	Wild flower areas
Knightshayes Court	●	●					●			●			●				●
Lacock Abbey	●		●	●			●				●		●		●		●
Lanhydrock	●	●					●			●	●		●				
Lavenham: The Guildhall of Corpus Christi							●										
Lindisfarne Castle							●		●				●				
Little Moreton Hall	●								●	●							
Llanerchaeron	●	●	●	●			●	●	●		●	●	●				●
Lyme Park	●			●			●			●	●		●	●			
Lytes Cary Manor		●					●						●				
Melford Hall			●	●									●				●
Mompesson House							●			●			●				
Monk's House													●	●			
Montacute House	●	●	●				●	●					●		●		
Moseley Old Hall	●	●	●					●					●				●
Mottisfont Abbey	●	●	●		●	●	●			●	●		●				●
Mottistone Manor					●	●	●	●	●				●				●
Mount Stewart	●	●		●						●	●		●				
Nostell Priory			●	●													
Nunnington Hall		●					●	●					●				●
Nymans Garden	●	●		●	●		●			●		●	●				●
Ormesby Hall	●		●	●			●						●				
Osterley Park			●											●			
Overbecks Garden	●									●			●	●			●
Oxburgh Hall	●			●					●				●				●
Packwood House	●	●			●		●						●				●
Peckover House	●			●			●		●				●		●		●
Penrhyn Castle	●			●						●			●				●
Petworth House	●	●								●			●				●
Plas Newydd	●			●	●	●				●	●		●				●
Plas Yn Rhiw		●	●							●			●				●
Polesden Lacey	●	●	●	●	●		●					●	●				●
Powis Castle	●	●	●	●			●			●	●	●	●		●		●
Prior Park			●								●					●	●
Rievaulx Terrace and Temples			●														●
Rowallane Garden	●		●	●						●		●	●	●			●
Rufford Old Hall	●	●		●			●		●				●				●
St Michael's Mount				●					●		●		●				●

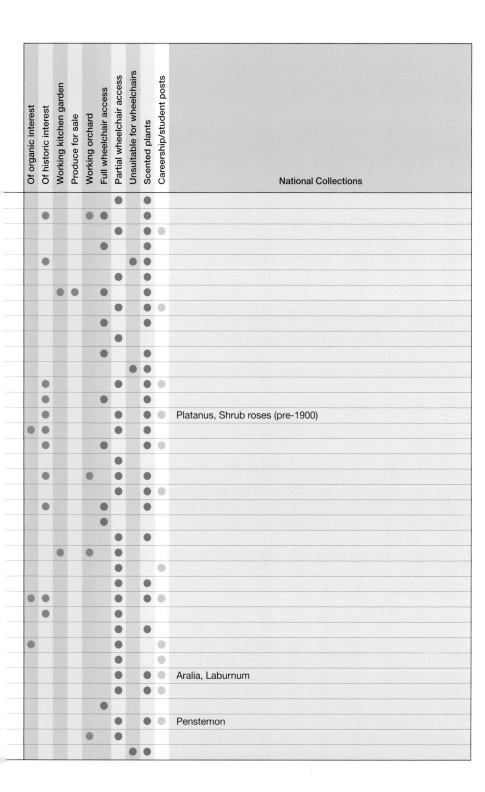

	Formal features	Topiary	Pre-Victorian landscape	Victorian/Edwardian features	Inter-war garden	Post-war garden	Rose garden/beds	Herb garden/borders	Fruit and vegetables	Rare trees and shrubs	Water garden	Rock garden	Herbaceous and mixed borders	Conservatory	Orangery	Grotto	Wild flower areas
Saltram		●								●			●		●		●
Scotney Castle		●	●				●	●		●	●		●				●
Shaw's Corner				●	●	●							●				●
Sheffield Park	●		●	●	●					●	●						
Shugborough	●	●	●	●			●						●				
Sissinghurst Castle	●			●				●					●				●
Sizergh Castle				●			●			●	●	●	●				●
Snowshill Manor				●				●	●				●				●
Speke Hall		●	●				●		●		●		●				●
Springhill								●					●				●
Stagshaw					●						●						
Standen			●				●					●	●				●
Stoneacre							●										
Stourhead		●	●					●		●	●					●	●
Stowe Landscape Gardens	●		●	●							●					●	●
Studley Royal Water Garden	●		●								●						
Sunnycroft				●			●		●			●	●				
Tatton Park	●	●	●	●			●	●		●	●	●	●	●	●		
Tintinhull House	●	●					●	●	●		●		●				
Trelissick			●	●			●	●	●	●			●				●
Trengwainton			●	●	●					●	●		●				
Trerice		●											●				
Upton House		●					●		●	●	●	●					●
The Vyne	●			●		●	●		●	●	●		●				●
Waddesdon Manor	●					●											
Wakehurst Place	●									●	●	●	●				●
Wallington	●		●	●		●					●		●	●			●
Washington Old Hall	●	●					●	●	●				●				●
The Weir	●	●									●	●					●
West Green House	●	●		●	●	●	●	●	●		●		●	●	●	●	●
West Wycombe Park		●									●						
Westbury Court	●	●							●	●							●
Wightwick Manor	●	●	●			●		●		●		●					●
Wimpole Hall	●	●	●	●						●	●						●
Winkworth Arboretum			●	●						●	●						●
	●	●					●	●	●		●		●				

Of organic interest	Of historic interest	Working kitchen garden	Produce for sale	Working orchard	Full wheelchair access	Partial wheelchair access	Unsuitable for wheelchairs	Scented plants	Careership/student posts	National Collections
					●			●		
					●			●		
●				●	●			●		
	●				●			●	○	Ghent Azalea
						●		●		
	●				●			●	○	
					●					
●					●			●		
					●			●	○	
					●			●		
							●			
					●			●		
						●	●	●		
					●			●	○	
							●			
					●					
		●		●	●			●		
	●	●	●	●				●		Adiantum
	●	●					●	●		
	●			●				●	○	Photinia, Azara
								●	○	
●		●		●				●		
		●	●					●	○	Asters
			●					●	○	
								●		
							●	●		Betula, Nothofagus, Skimmia, Hypericum
							●	●		Sambucus
	●						●	●		
								●		
			●				●	●		
								●		
		●	●	●				●		
					●				○	
	●	●	●		●				○	Walnut trees
							●	●		Sorbus
	●	●		●	●					

Maps

The key opposite shows how England, Wales and Northern Ireland are divided into 11 areas for the purposes of this Handbook and displayed on seven maps. The maps show those properties which have individual entries as well as those which are mentioned briefly in the area introduction. Please note that the map for London is incorporated within that covering the South East.

In order to help with general orientation, the maps show main roads and population centres. However, the plotting of each site serves only as a guide to its location. Please note that some countryside properties, eg. those in the Lake District, cover many thousands of hectares. In such cases the symbol is placed centrally as an indication of general location.

Key:		
Map 1		South West
Map 2		South and South East
		London
Map 3		East of England
		East Midlands
Map 4		Wales
		West Midlands
Map 5		Yorkshire
		North West
Map 6		North West
		North East
Map 7		Northern Ireland

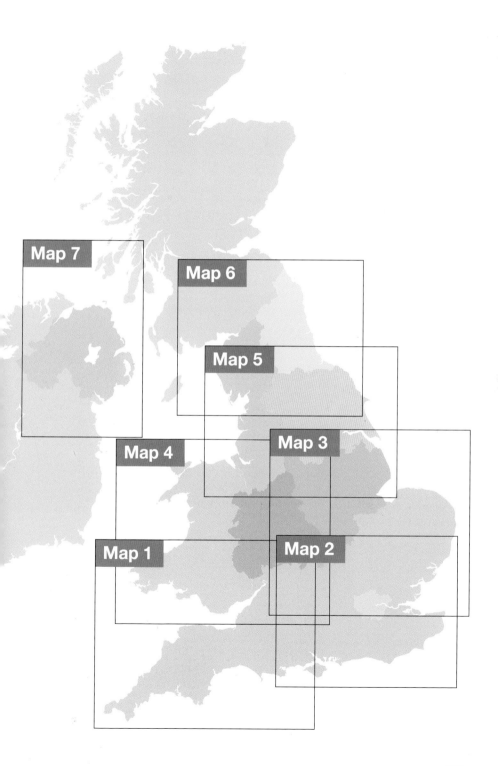

Map 7

Map 6

Map 5

Map 3

Map 4

Map 1

Map 2

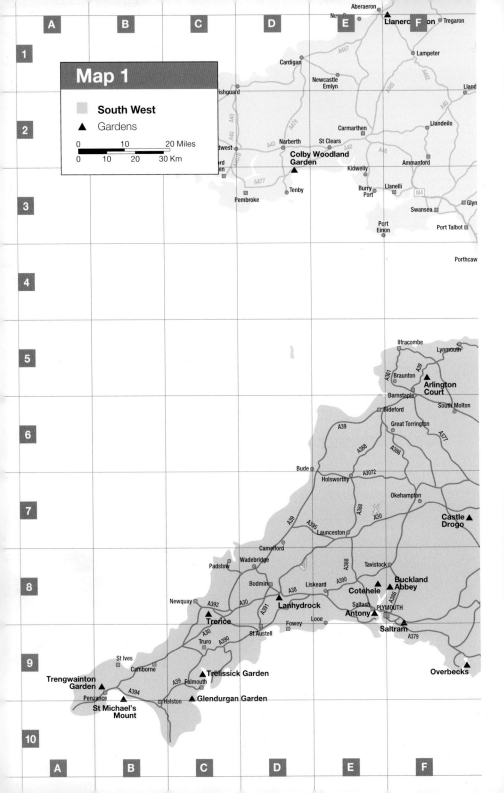

Map 1

South West

▲ Gardens

0	10		20 Miles
0	10	20	30 Km

Aberaeron

Ne... Llanerc F on Tregaron

Lampeter

A487

Cardigan

Newcastle
Emlyn

...ishguard Lland

Carmarthen Llandeilo

Narberth St Clears

...dwest **Colby Woodland
Garden** ▲

...rd Kidwelly Ammanford

...en

A477

Tenby Burry Llanelli

Pembroke Port M4 Glyn

Swansea

Port
Einon Port Talbot

Porthcaw

Ilfracombe

Lynmouth

Braunton **Arlington
Court** ▲

Barnstaple

Bideford South Molton

A39 Great Torrington

A388 A386

Bude

Holsworthy A3072

Okehampton

A388 A30

A39 A395 **Castle ▲
Drogo**

Launceston

Camelford

Wadebridge A388 Tavistock

Padstow **Buckland ▲
Abbey**

Bodmin Liskeard A390 **Cotehele** ▲

Newquay A392 A38 Saltash PLYMOUTH

A30 **Lanhydrock** Antony ▲

A381 Fowey Looe

Trerice ▲ **Saltram** ▲

A30 St Austell A379

Truro A390

St Ives

Camborne **Overbecks** ▲

**Trengwainton
Garden** ▲ **Trelissick Garden** ▲

Penzance A39 Falmouth A394

**St Michael's
Mount** ▲ Helston **Glendurgan Garden** ▲

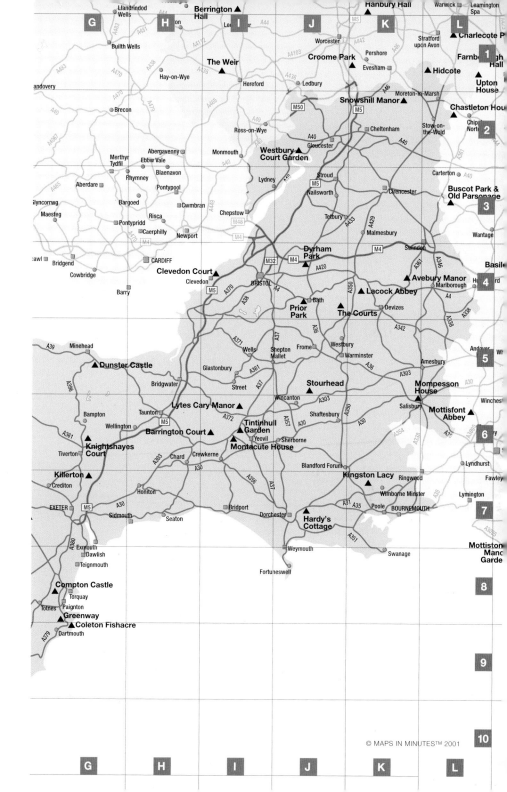

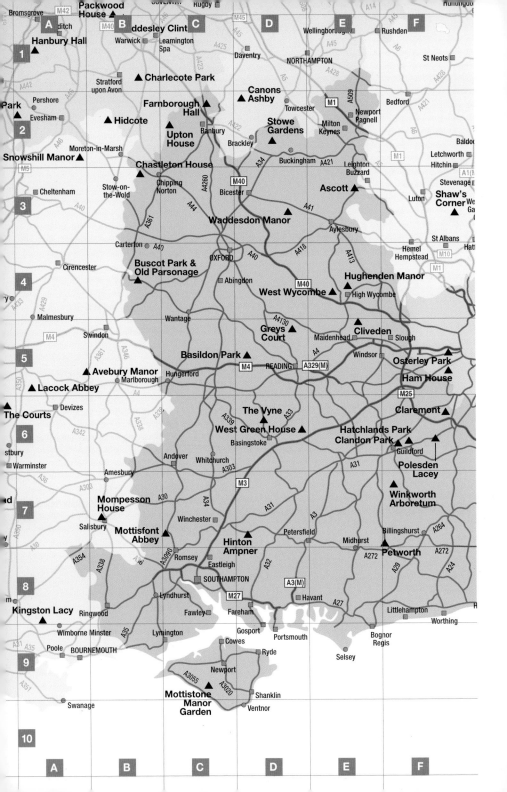

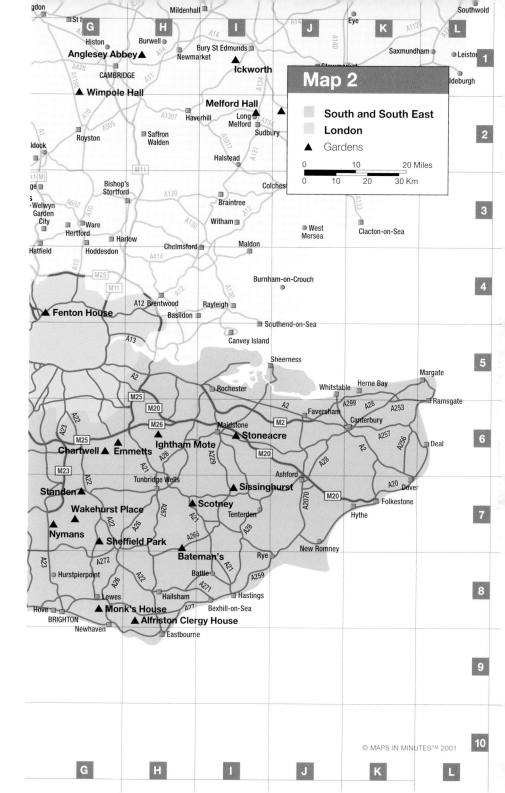

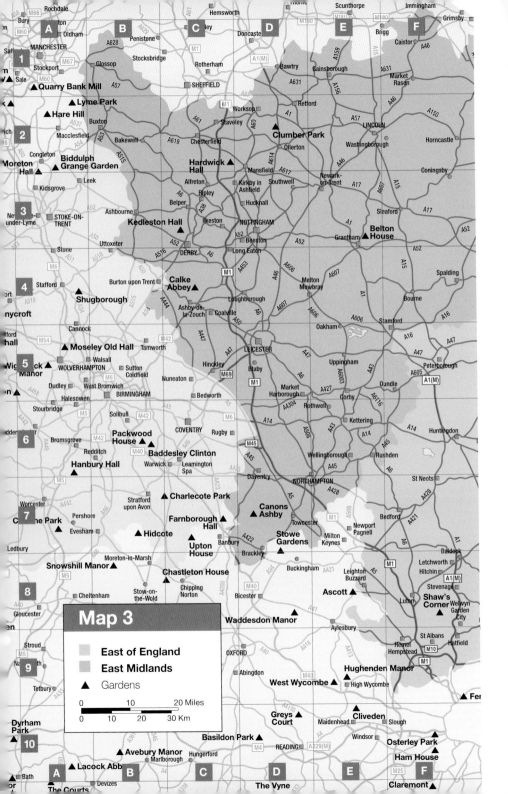

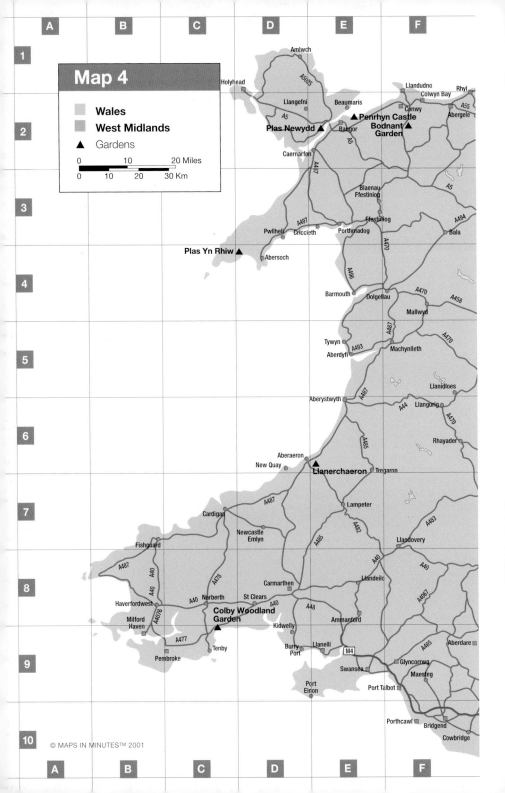

Map 4

Wales
West Midlands
▲ Gardens

0   10   20 Miles
0   10   20   30 Km

Amlwch
Holyhead
A5025
Llandudno
Colwyn Bay
Rhyl
Llangefni
Beaumaris
Conwy
A55
Abergele
A5
Penrhyn Castle
Plas Newydd ▲
Bangor
Bodnant ▲
Garden
A5
Caernarfon
A487
Blaenau
Ffestiniog
A5
A497
Ffestiniog
A494
Pwllheli
Criccieth
Porthmadog
Bala
Plas Yn Rhiw ▲
Abersoch
A470
A496
Barmouth
Dolgellau
A470
A458
Mallwyd
A487
A470
Tywyn
A493
Machynlleth
Aberdyfi
Llanidloes
A487
Aberystwyth
A44
Llangurig
A470
A485
Rhayader
Aberaeron
New Quay
▲ Llanerchaeron
Tregaron
A487
Lampeter
A483
Cardigan
A482
Newcastle
Emlyn
A485
Llandovery
Fishguard
A40
A40
A487
A40
A40
Llandeilo
A40
A478
Carmarthen
A467
Haverfordwest
A40
Narberth
St Clears
A40
A40/76
Milford
Haven
Colby Woodland
Garden
A48
Ammanford
A477
Kidwelly
Burry
Port
Llanelli
A465
Aberdare
Pembroke
Tenby
M4
Port
Eirion
Swansea
Glyncorrwg
Maesteg
Port Talbot
Porthcawl
Bridgend
Cowbridge

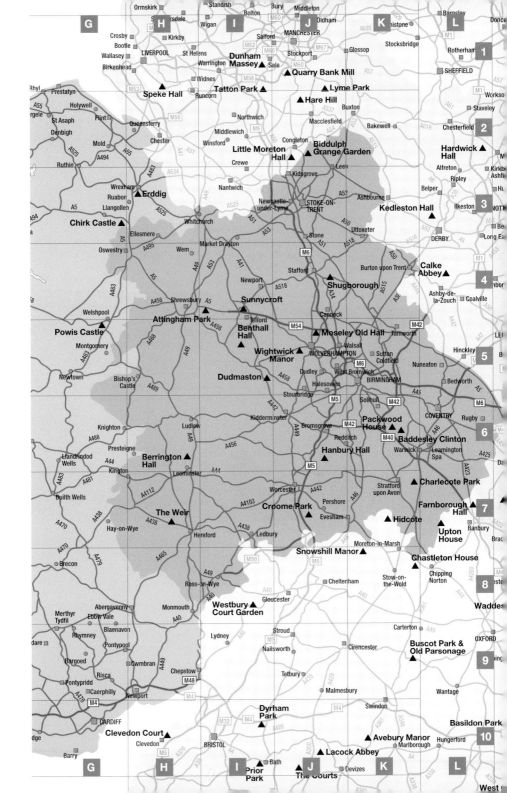

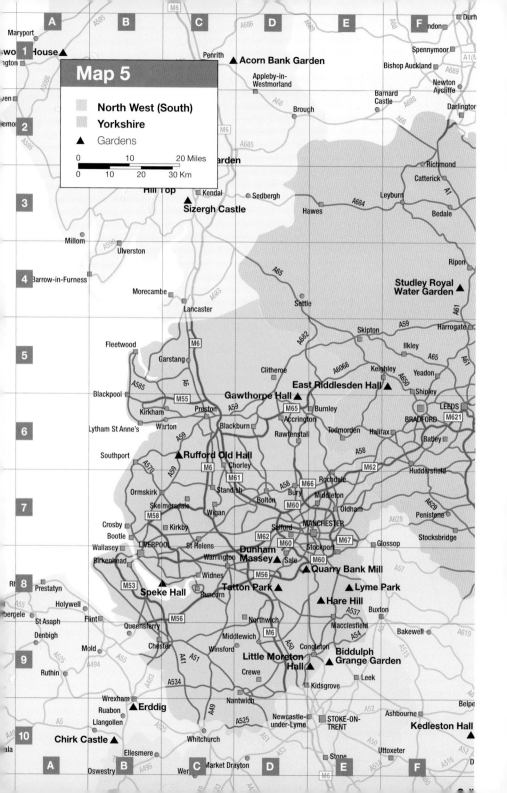

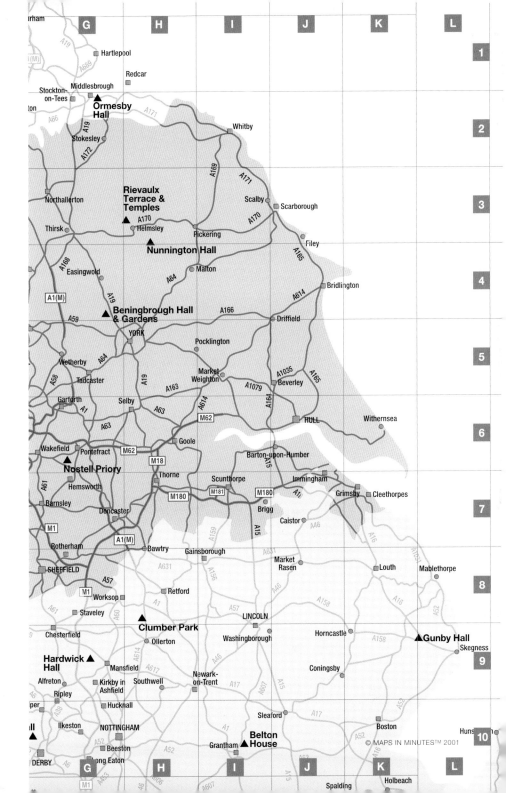

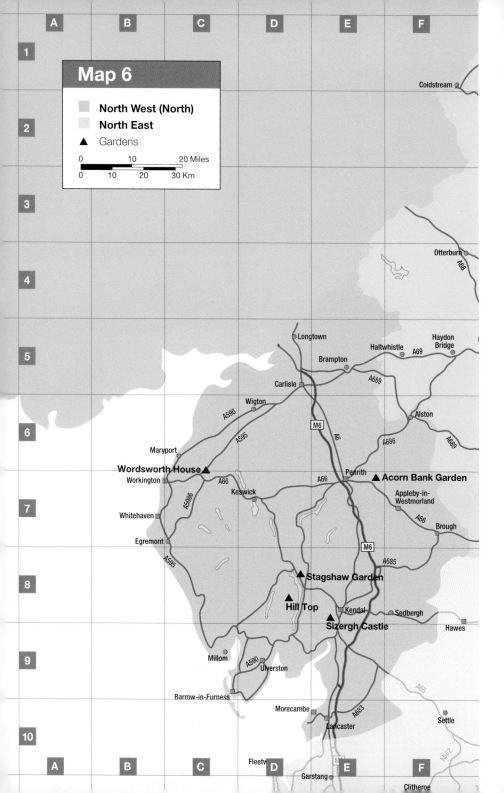

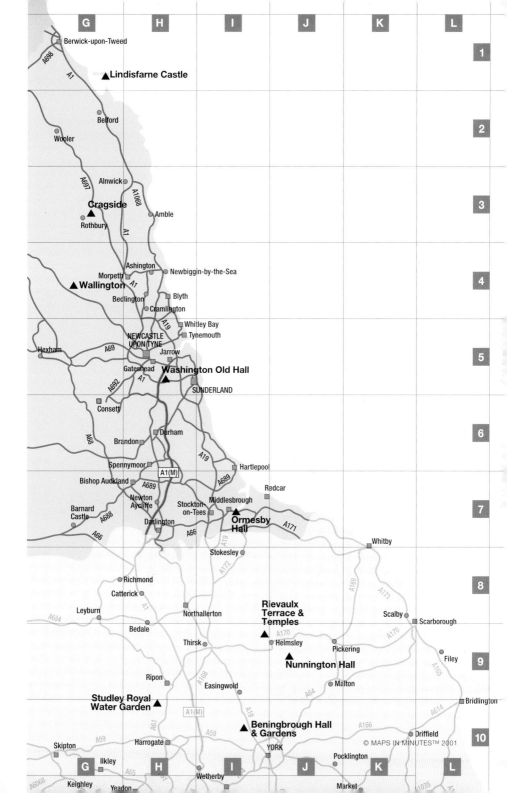

The National Trust for Scotland

The National Trust for Scotland, a charity like the National Trust but an entirely separate body, is Scotland's leading conservation organisation.

With more than 283 hectares under intensive cultivation, the NTS is the country's largest garden owner. The Trust acquired its first garden in 1945 at Culzean Castle in Ayrshire; seven years later Inverewe, Brodick Castle, Falkland Palace and Pitmedden Gardens were added to a developing portfolio which now includes 34 major gardens and designed landscapes and about 30 smaller gardens.

Almost every style of Scottish garden history is represented – late-medieval at Culross Palace; Victorian formality at Haddo House and House of Dun; early 20th-century plant-rich collections at Arduaine, Branklyn and Inverewe; and modern creations in older settings such as Inveresk Lodge and Priorwood.

The Trust also promotes the art and craft of practical gardening – be it through maintaining the 300-year-old topiary hedges at Crathes Castle, or through the student training provided at its School of Practical Gardening at Threave.

For more information contact The National Trust for Scotland, Wemyss House, 28 Charlotte Square, Edinburgh EH2 4ET, tel (0131) 243 9300; or visit the website at **www.nts.org.uk**

How you can support the National Trust
BECOME A MEMBER TODAY

You will be helping the Trust protect and care for much-loved countryside and coastline as well as historic houses and gardens. Your subscription goes directly to support this work. Benefits include:

- free admission to most properties listed

- three mailings a year which include a free copy of the annual Handbook, three editions of the full colour *National Trust Magazine* (available also on tape) and two editions of your regional newsletter

There is a wide range of different membership categories for you to choose from.

How to join

For immediate membership, you can join at almost all National Trust properties or shops during your visit, or join on-line at **www.nationaltrust.org.uk/join**

Or just telephone the National Trust Membership Department on 0870 458 4000. Enquiries and credit card applications are welcome. The lines are open Monday to Friday 9 am to 5.30 pm and from 9 am to 4 pm on Saturdays, Sundays and Bank Holidays (except Christmas Day and New Year's Day). Please allow 21 days for receipt of your membership card and new member's pack.

How you can support the National Trust in the USA
JOIN THE ROYAL OAK FOUNDATION

More than 40,000 Americans belong to the Royal Oak Foundation, the Trust's US membership affiliate. A not-for-profit organisation, the Royal Oak helps the National Trust through the generous tax-deductible support of members and friends by making grants towards its work. Member benefits include the National Trust Handbook, three editions of *The National Trust Magazine*, the quarterly Royal Oak Newsletter, and free admission to properties of the National Trust and of the National Trust for Scotland.

Royal Oak also awards scholarships to US residents to study in Britain, and sponsors lectures, tours and events in both the US and the UK, designed to inform Americans of the Trust's work.

For further information please write, call, fax or email
The Royal Oak Foundation, 26 Broadway,
Suite 950, New York, NY 10004, USA
tel. **001 212 480 2889**
fax **001 212 785 7234**
email **general@royal-oak.org**
web **www.royal-oak.org**